Set Free

A Journey Toward
Solidarity Against Racism

Iris de León-Hartshorn
Tobin Miller Shearer
Regina Shands Stoltzfus

Foreword by Ched Myers

Herald
Press

Scottdale, Pennsylvania
Waterloo, Ontario

Library of Congress Cataloging-in-Publication Data
León-Hartshorn, Iris de, 1951
    Set free : a journey toward solidarity against racism / Iris de
León-Hartshorn, Tobin Miller Shearer, Regina Shands Stoltzfus.
    p. cm.
    Includes bibliographical references.
    ISBN 0-8361-9157-9 (alk. paper)
    1. United States—Race relations. 2. Racism—United States—
Psychological aspects. 3. Racism—Religious aspects—Christianity.
4. Race relations—Religious aspects—Christianity. 5. Race
relations—Handbooks, manuals, etc. 6. Church and social
problems—United states. I. Shearer, Tobin Miller, 1965-
II. Stoltzfus, Regina Shands, 1959- III. Title.

E185.615 .L466 2001
305.8'00973—dc21   2001024367

SET FREE
Copyright © 2001 by Herald Press, Scottdale, Pa. 15683
    Published simultaneously in Canada by Herald Press,
    Waterloo, Ont. N2L 6H7. All rights reserved
Library of Congress Catalog Card Number: 2001024367
International Standard Book Number: 0-8361-9157-9
Printed in the United States of America
Book design by Jim Butti
Cover art and design by Gwen M. Stamm

10 09 08 07 06 05 04 03 02 01   10 9 8 7 6 5 4 3 2 1

To order or request information, please call 1-800-759-4447 (individuals); 1-800-245-7894 (trade). Website: www.mph.org

To Matthew, Danny, Rachel, and Joshua—may you always thank God for who you are and never be afraid to be just that—who you are. RSS

To Andres, Isabel, and Toni—may you see yourselves as God created you, in the image of the Creator. IDH

To Dylan and Zachary—may you learn from my mistakes. TMS

Contents

Foreword

Crazy Horse, it says in my American Heritage, *was "killed while resisting arrest." Lies can make you crazy faster than anything else. This is not the first lie I have discovered in the dictionary, but I wish it was the last. What would the last lie look like? How would it feel? Would we miss lies if we didn't have them? Living with lies is a shattering experience. The dictionary tells us the root for craze is* krasa, *Old Norse meaning to shatter. This is not a lie.*
    —*Christina V. Pacosz,* Some Winded, Wild Beast

The authors of *Set Free: A Journey Toward Solidarity Against Racism* advocate that we must all contribute to the struggle to "melt the iceberg of racism." Similarly, Christina Pacosz concludes her reflection on the shattering impact of lies: "We must chase them to the sun, again and again, no matter how tired we think we are . . . until all the lies in the world are herded together and burned up." These two metaphors couldn't be more appropriate. Fire and ice are the two oldest elements humans have used for treating their most serious wounds.

Racism is truly our "hidden wound" in North America, as Wendell Berry put it in his book by that name. To ignore or to bandage this wound cosmetically is simply to ensure it will fester—surely the twentieth century proved that. Racism can only be healed by the painful but cleansing fire and ice of the truth. And if we do not speak the truth—about both the past and the present of racism—then we must deal with a very different kind of fire and ice. For history shows us repeatedly that the "cold war" of frozen race relations inevitably erupts into the heat of built-up rage. James Baldwin warned of this very thing in his famous 1963 ultimatum, *The Fire Next Time:*

> We may be able, handful that we are, to end the racial nightmare, and achieve our country and change the history of the world. If we do not now dare everything, the fulfillment of that prophecy, recreated from the Bible in song by a slave, is upon us: "God gave Noah the rainbow sign; no more water, the fire next time!"

The writers of this volume know all too well the "chilly" reception that usually awaits attempts to address racism in our workplaces, in our neighborhoods, and even and especially in our churches. And I, for one, have watched my city burn twice in my lifetime because of the persistent violence and dehumanization of racism and our refusal to have a public conversation about it (I write today on the ninth anniversary of the 1992 Los Angeles uprising, the largest "civil disturbance" in U.S. history).

Fortunately, Regina Shands Stoltzfus, Iris de León-Hartshorn, and Tobin Miller Shearer understand that we cannot responsibly speak about racism and its legacy without simultaneously addressing the fire and ice of both healing and judgment. They have thus produced a volume that will encourage and equip all those who wish to learn how to have truthful conversations about racism that heal. The stories, concepts, biblical metaphors, and practical challenges woven into these chapters venture both deep and wide in articulating the many dimensions of racism, as well as the work required to "melt the iceberg." Personal accounts stand side by side with clear analysis, inviting us to reflect critically on our own experiences of violation, ambivalence, denial, or liberation.

Above all, the authenticity of this project lies in the fact that it arises from the practice behind it. All three authors have been deeply involved in antiracism education and advocacy work for many years. The insights and approaches narrated in this book have been forged in workshops, congregations, and institutions around the country. Moreover, Iris, Regina, and Tobin worked as a team in writing this book, as reflected in the way their diverse viewpoints have been expressed with symmetry and coherency. This means that they had to work out among themselves the very issues they address. The fact that they model the process they write about is the book's highest commendation. I encourage readers to work through this book in that spirit: as a group that can explore this same process of being "set free" by the journey toward solidarity.

As Mennonites, the authors stand in the great Anabaptist tradition of peacemaking and gospel witness against all forms of domination. They address this book primarily to churches in full knowledge, however, that most North American congregations (including Mennonites) still balk at engaging in this conversation. But if Christians can't embrace among ourselves the truth of racism in all of its fire and ice, how can we expect to nurture a public conversation? And if there is no public conversation, how can we hope for social reconciliation?

Conversely, the courageous experience of the Truth and Reconciliation commission in post-apartheid South Africa (under the leadership of the churches) shows the dramatic transformational power of public truth-telling. It is up to those who profess faith to work with God's Spirit to help melt the iceberg: "God sends the Word that melts the frost, stirs up the breezes, and the waters flow" (Psalm 147:18). Followers of the One who called himself the Truth must help chase the lies to the sun: "Everyone will be salted with fire. . . . Have salt in yourselves, then, and be at peace" (Mark 9:49-50).

The task is no less urgent today than when James Baldwin wrote. The lies of racism continue to make us all "crazy," whether we are privileged by or disadvantaged by our skin color, whether we have spoken up or kept silent, whether we imagine ourselves a victim or an innocent. Our society and our church have been "shattered" by these lies. The truth alone can put us together again.

Ched Myers
Bartimaeus Cooperative Ministries
Los Angeles, California
May 2001

Preface

The first answer this book offers is that racism is a name-caller. The final question it poses is, "So what?" Somewhere between that first cryptic answer and the surly query that follows, we hope you will find words worth reading and insight worth taking on your journey.

We do hope, and yet we are cautious in that hope. We do not come as experts in the writing. Neither do we come as strugglers from the grassroots. Rather, we are a group of three, connected to a national Mennonite service agency, who have been blessed with the space, support, and opportunity to take time to reflect on our small part of the antiracism struggle. It is neither the only part, nor the most significant, but it is the one into which we have been called to enter. We aim to share insight from that struggle here.

Even as we recognize the small size of our offering, we are also aware of the power of printed words. Particularly in book form, they amplify and extend the weight and significance of the perspectives written down. By contrast, oral traditions rarely carry such weight in this information age. And so our hope that these pages hold some worthwhile insight is further tempered by our recognition that what we write here has certainly been said by others elsewhere. We are deeply grateful for what we have learned from the many teachers and co-strugglers who have entered our lives in profound ways.

We also write as members of specific communities. While together we represent the broad racial groupings of African-

American, Latino, and white, we also bring specific regional experiences from the Southwest, West Coast, East Coast, and Great Lakes. Likewise, we write as women and a man, mothers and a father, daughters and a son, wives and a husband. Most importantly we want to be clear that, while we will make systemic observations throughout this book, our voices do not represent all people of color groups or the breath of national identities that racism continues to mold into whiteness.

Our aim in this work is to focus on the identity-shaping power of racism. We will work to describe the two primary forms this level of racism takes: internalized racist oppression (IRO) and internalized racist superiority (IRS). For this reason, we say we start with the answer that racism is a name-caller. For we who are white, racism calls out "racist." For we who are people of color, racism calls out "victim." In our experience, we all have been taught to believe the names racism speaks.

We begin by focusing on internalized racist oppression. Regina and Iris have written three chapters each that explore the systemic and personal ramifications of internalized oppression among Aboriginal, African-American, Latino, and Asian communities in the United States. Following those six chapters, Tobin has written three additional chapters exploring the realities of internalized racist superiority as expressed in white people.

We have chosen to give more space to the discussion of internalized racist oppression because currently there are far fewer written resources focusing on this reality than on the realities of white privilege, power, and superiority. But, we have also chosen to write about both themes in one book because we are committed to the principle of people of color and white people struggling together to dismantle racism. Every team that is trained through our Mennonite and Brethren in Christ based antiracism program, Damascus Road, is required to reflect that racial balance. Likewise, we never agree to conduct a workshop or training unless our training team reflects a similar racial and gender mix.

The final four chapters bring the theory and reflection of the first nine chapters down to a practical level as we write about ways to respond to the "So what?" question. We look specifically at what white people need from people of color in solidarity relationships, what people of color need from white people, where opportunities have been missed, and finally, where opportunities to engage in antiracist action have been taken.

The stories you will encounter here come from our lives. We have tried to be as vulnerable and transparent as we can be in the telling. In the seven years that we have worked together there have been many tears shed, mistakes made, and disagreements discovered. Likewise, we have laughed long, worshiped deeply, and just hung out. We hope both realities are reflected in the stories that we tell.

In order to understand these stories and our focus on the name-calling nature of racism, we want to make clear a number of assumptions we bring to this exploration.

The first is that we write as Christians. We are sustained and strengthened in our work to dismantle racism through our faith in a loving God and our belief in the example, ministry, and resurrection of Jesus Christ. We live and experience that belief as members of Mennonite congregations where we draw from a long tradition of resisting and naming as evil all powers that seek to deal death in this world.

Christian belief also informs our understanding of the nature of racism. More than anything else, we are convinced that racism is a demon. Or, to use less dramatic language, we understand racism to be a principality and power that is made manifest in the world in which we live. Thus, racism is not simply a force that can be broken down into quantified chunks through the tools that sociology, psychology, anthropology, and political science offer us. While we find those tools helpful and readily use them, we believe that racism is, at its root, sin and thus holds spiritual dimensions that science cannot describe.

A third assumption we bring to this book is that racism is not the same as racial prejudice. Where racial prejudice is held by many of us regardless of our skin color, racism is only present when a given racial group in society has the power to enforce their racial prejudices so that they receive more benefits and privileges than other groups. Because we have found it to be such a helpful tool in establishing a common language and paradigm to work together across racial lines, we use a definition of racism common to many antiracism groups in this country: Racism = race prejudice + misuse of systemic power.

Racism, however, is not as one-dimensional as this definition suggests. It can be found in three primary manifestations: individual, institutional, and systemic. Likewise, each of those manifestations has three levels: Oppressive Power, White Power, and Identity Power.[1] And so, our next assumption is that racism is an iceberg.

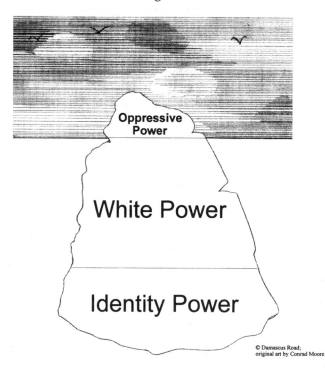

© Damascus Road;
original art by Conrad Moore

As the diagram on the opposite page suggests, most often we only see the tip of the iceberg, or Oppressive Power. This is the level of racism at which people of color are harmed whether individually, institutionally, or systemically. Most often, and especially for white people and society, we only know that racism is a bad thing for people of color. While afloat on the multicultural boat, we work hard to avoid doing bad things to people of color. Usually it is white people who control the steering, and as they design programs to meet this level of racism, they only know to avoid what they see, the tip of the iceberg. The other 9/10ths of the iceberg go unnoticed.

Examples of Oppressive Power include:

- Overt physical or verbal attacks on people of color such as the June 1998 murder of James Byrd Jr., when he was dragged to his death behind a pickup truck in Jasper, Texas (individual manifestation).
- Redlining policies that prohibit the distribution of housing loans, taxicab service, newspaper delivery, police protection, and pizza delivery to communities of color (institutional manifestation).
- The practice of "killing the Indian to save the man" as expressed in Bureau of Indian Affairs Boarding schools where aboriginal children were removed from their parents and communities, forced to speak English, shorn, stripped of culture, and shamed into denouncing their people (systemic manifestation).

Beneath the surface of the water is the next level of the racism iceberg. At the level of White Power, we discover the core or purpose of racism to be that white people and society are given power and privilege. This is the bulk of the berg and is the part most difficult for white people to see. White Power is what most often goes entirely unnoticed by those steering the multicultural boat of white-controlled institutions. It is here that we examine the countless ways white people receive power and privilege through individual, institutional, and systemic forces.

Examples of White Power include:

- The many times Tobin has received the bill for a restaurant meal when the party included both men and women of color, some of whom were his direct supervisors, as well as the myriad ways white people receive quicker service, less harassment, more inclusion, and fewer negative messages in course of daily life at work, in public space, during school, and while at recreation (individual manifestations).

- An institutional policy to allow staff to listen only to "Christian, classical, or easy-listening music" in the office environment and then to enforce that policy according to white-defined examples of those music styles, as well as any time an institution decides to develop policies based on white norms, standards, and values (institutional manifestations).

- Walt Disney's repeated use of light-skinned, European-featured characters as the heroes of movies like *Pocahontas, El Dorado, Hercules,* etc., as well as the repeated and overwhelming equation of beauty with white examples in popular culture magazines, movies, and television shows (systemic manifestations).

There is yet another level of the racism iceberg. This third level, Identity Power, is where we must have a theological lens to understand the power of racism as it attempts to shape our identities. It is here that we see how racism tries to usurp God's authority to tell us who we are. As racists and victims are shaped by racism, the two topics of this book come into focus: internalized racist oppression and internalized racist superiority. This book attempts to go deep below the surface of the water and examine the bottom of the berg. Again we will look at all the manifestations or sides of this level: individual, institutional, and systemic.

Examples of Identity Power include:

- Any Horatio Alger story, or the many others like it, that portray white people "pulling themselves up by their bootstraps" and believing that they have done it by themselves (IRS), or the funeral plans of some young gang members of color who do not believe they will reach adulthood (IRO) (individual manifestations).

- The involvement of people of color in institutions that are overtly oppressing other people of color such as border patrol agents at the Mexican-American border (IRO), or the proliferation of white-led, controlled, and designed short-term mission programs that are far more focused on the needs of the white sending agency than the communities of color in which they so often operate with no identifiable accountability (IRS) (institutional manifestations).

- When some Native churches reject indigenous forms of worship, refusing to believe that ways of knowing, communicating, or worshiping stemming from their communities are just as valid as white ways of doing the same (IRO), or the appropriation of African-American, Latino, Native, or Asian culture by white people as their own, as exemplified in contemporary advertising campaigns such as the way in which Kentucky Fried Chicken has turned Colonel Sanders, an icon of the plantation South, into a caricature of a black man (systemic manifestations).

As we indicated above, we will expand, in particular, on the examples and themes of Identity Power in the first nine chapters of this book. The final four chapters deal with all levels and manifestation of the iceberg in an integrated form.

Our fifth and final assumption is that, while we will always have sin to struggle with in this fallen world, we are convinced that we can melt the iceberg of racism. If nothing else, we are called to this task as children of God who live in a sinful world. We do not pretend that the work will be easy, short-term, or without significant setbacks—even failures. We are struggling with a demonic power, but one that Christ has already overcome. We pray that these pages might be of encouragement and direction as we together answer the call to resist racism in this world.

We have many thanks to offer those who have been of support to us in this undertaking. First, we offer praise and thanksgiving to God, our provider and source of strength, for calling us to this task. Second, we want to thank our families for their willingness to see us through this project and the work of antiracism that so often takes us away from home. With deep appreciation, love, and honor, we thank you Andres, Art, Cheryl, Danny, Dylan, Isabele, Leo, Matthew, Joshua, Rachel, Toni, and Zachary.

To our many other reviewers, encouragers, supporters, and listeners we also offer thanks: Michelle Armster, Phil Brubaker, Jeff Gingerich, Linda Goertz, Lee Heights Community Church, Dody Matthias, Conrad Moore, Ched Myers, Louise Stoltzfus, Mennonite Central Committee U.S., Sharon Williams, and Brenda Zook Friesen.

A special thanks to our editors, Byron Rempel-Burkholder and Sarah Kehrberg for sticking with us through this process.

Peace,

> Iris de León-Hartshorn
> Tobin Miller Shearer
> Regina Shands Stoltzfus
> February 2001

1

Naming the Problem

O Lord, you have searched me and you know me.
You know when I sit and when I rise;
* you perceive my thoughts from afar. . . .*
You hem me in—behind and before; you have laid your
* hand upon me. . . .*
For you created my inmost being;
* you knit me together in my mother's womb.*
I praise you because I am fearfully and wonderfully made;
* your works are wonderful, I know that full well.*
(Psalm 139:1-2; 5; 13-14 NIV)

In 1790, a group of five free biracial men in Charleston, South Carolina, formed a social club called the Brown Fellowship Society. The society, with its color restrictions (a certain degree of lightness was required) and $50 membership fee was meant to appeal to an elite group of light-skinned men who wished to establish a social position similar to the white aristocracy. Membership later opened to women, but continued to restrict dark-skinned people. In response to this discrimination within the race, a group limited to those with a certain degree of darkness was formed: the Free Dark Men of Color.

My mother, a dark-skinned woman, remembers her high school years in the 1940s being tainted by "colorism." In her all-black high school in Miami, Florida, every position voted on by classmates was won by students who were light-skinned. Merit placements, however, came in all shades. Clearly, the students were expressing their preference for one group above the other. I remember her teaching kids (including my brother) who were teased by others for being dark the old retort, "the blacker the berry, the sweeter the juice." My own children range in shades from very dark to very light. I remember my oldest son's devastation when at five, he found out he was not "white" regardless of how light his skin is.[1] My only daughter has wished for light skin and straight hair. The pattern repeats itself generation after generation.

Internalized racist oppression is, at its simplest, people of color believing the lie that we are *less than* because we are not white. Racism lies to us, saying we are less intelligent, less beautiful, less capable, and less worthy because we are African-American, Latino/a or Hispanic, Native American, Asian American, Arab American, or Pacific Islanders. Internalized racist oppression is understanding that basic lie to be true, and then living it out. The *less-than* lie comes from many directions: home, school, the workplace, and the media, to name a few.

Internalized racist oppression comes from being stopped for being the wrong color in the wrong neighborhood. It is borne out of being followed in stores because of suspicion of theft, strip-searched in airports because of suspicion of smuggling drugs. Internalized racist oppression develops from leafing through magazines and seeing page after page of only happy white people. It is higher sentencing rates and more severe punishments for the same or lesser crimes committed by white people.

Day after day, over and over again, people of color are bombarded with messages that say "you don't count (at least not as much as white people)," and the cumulative effect of these messages becomes internalized. Internalized racist oppression has many manifestations and has ingrained itself into aspects of our cultural lives. It shows up in the jokes we tell, the myths we create and perpetrate, and some family system patterns. While some of these patterns have been helpful coping strategies and survival techniques, for the most part internalized racist oppression has serious ramifications for our individual physical, mental, and spiritual healthiness, and for the survival of our communities.

The most serious consequence of the effects of internalized racist oppression is that our understanding of ourselves as created beings who in some way bear the stamp of the divine essentially disappears. The creation account in Genesis tells us that "God created humanity in God's own image . . . male and female they were created." For Christians, knowing that we have been created *in* the image of God, *for* God's own glory, is a primary understanding of humankind's relationship with God. God so loved this creation that a Savior was sent to redeem us that we might forever dwell with our Creator. Clearly, humanity is important to God—all of humanity. Yet, the most fundamental way in which racism reaches its goal of upholding white supremacy and superiority is to dehumanize people of color. And so, instead of human beings, Africans became animal-like brutes for whom slavery was a destiny. The people who inhabited the land that became known as North, Central, and South America became godless savages who didn't deserve the land, making forcible takeover of that land acceptable by any means necessary, up to and including genocide. The legacies of slavery and colonization have created generations of people who have lived under the physical reality of people of color being subjugated to white people. That physical reality cannot help but impact the internal sense of self: "If whites are not truly better than people of color, then why are they in control of everything? Why are their neighborhoods clean and well-planned out and my neighborhood is chaotic and lacks services? Why do their schools have the latest technologies, and my school doesn't even have enough books? Why are their children thriving, and more of my children in prison than in college?"

The gains of the civil rights era make such questions even more difficult to answer. Slavery has been abolished, Jim Crow laws are a thing of the past, and the wholesale physical slaughter of Native Americans has ended. Discrimination and hate crimes are illegal. According to the law, the playing field has been leveled and each person has equal opportunity. However, changing the law (for which we are grateful) does not erase the effects of the past five centuries. We have observed that although the law has changed, racism, like a virus, has mutated to adapt to the current times. Legalized, overt racism is a thing of the past, but racism itself has not gone away—it has gone underground. And like the racism of old, the racism of today sustains itself on the internalization of racist oppression and racist superiority. Carter G. Woodson, an African-American who was concerned about accurate knowledge of history and is known as the Father of Black History for his contributions, wrote in his book *The Mis-education of the Negro*:

> When you control a man's thinking you do not have to worry about his actions. You do not have to tell him to stand here or go yonder. He will find his "proper place" and will stay in it. You do not need to send him to the back door. He will go without being told. In fact, if there is no back door, he will cut one for his special benefit.[2]

It is important to note that the phenomenon of internalized racist oppression is not simply about low self-esteem; any person of any color can have low self-esteem. In fact, many people of color have high self-esteem but still suffer under the effects of the internalization process. Good programs have been created to raise the sense of self and the self-esteem of children of color, and have had successful results. And yet, internalized oppression remains a reality because the system of racism keeps it in place. Individual will cannot affect a systemic reality—the system itself must be addressed. As long as racism exists, its by-products, internalized racist oppression and internalized racist superiority, continue.

How is this possible?

I have good memories of my childhood. My parents were part of the Great Migration in the 1940s and 50s when blacks left the south primarily for economic reasons, but also to escape segregation. North of the Ohio River, the free states had long been a better place for blacks to find jobs, physical safety for their families, and educational opportunities for their children. After two years of living in the inner city, my parents bought a house in the southeast corner of Cleveland in a relatively new neighborhood that was being formed in a previously wooded area. Called "the island" by the people who lived there, it was still bounded on three sides by woods, and the fourth boundary was a railroad track that physically separated us from the rest of the city. To do anything—shop, bank, go to work, or go to school—we had to cross the tracks. To the mostly rural, southern adults who moved into that neighborhood, the surrounding woods made this the area of the city that seemed most like that from which they had come. Inside our borders we lived a completely black existence, with black expressions and ways of being. It was a good street to grow up on: neighbors were concerned about each other and the children belonged to the neighborhood. If you did something wrong on one end of the street, the news of it reached your household before you did. Like neighborhoods of color all over the country, such a place was more than a residence, it was a haven. Living in the United States, which was still undergoing massive racial unrest and upheaval during my growing-up years in the sixties and seventies, the island was a place to be free to be black.

Even so, within this haven there was also an ever-present awareness of the surrounding whiteness of the larger universe. With that awareness came the message of whiteness as rightness. We were smart enough to know this was not true, we had parents and teachers and preachers who told us all people were indeed equal, and yet there was enough supporting evidence to at least make us question it from time to time. White people rarely touched our world except in the forms of "official" people coming to do business: the insurance man, the milkman, and the police. Even as we were told we were beautiful, smart children, we knew the world thought otherwise. A major part of this understanding came simply from observing black representation, or the lack of it. When I was growing up, a black person on television was a major event, a call-your-friends-and-neighbors kind of event. Mainstream media like billboards, magazines, and books offered up "whiteness" as the norm. Most images of people of color came only in the worst stereotypes like the shuffling, clueless yet entertaining Negro, the savage (or noble savage) Indian, or the shiftless, lazy Mexican.

We could also see the physical difference in the things that belonged to us and the things that belonged to whites. For instance, the street I lived on until I was 18 years old was not paved until after I left home in the late 70s. Our schools were overcrowded and run down. White people moved away from the neighborhoods blacks moved into. My mother remembers living with the fear that a fire or some other emergency would occur while a train was stopped on the tracks, preventing any emergency assistance from coming through. Although we did not live under Jim Crow segregation in the North, we still lived segregated lives, and we knew about the signs that said "no colored" in the places our parents had come from. We knew about the riots that were happening all over the country and in our own city. Going to the South to visit relatives always involved careful preparation. We had to have food enough to last the trip because there would be few places to stop and eat, bathrooms were not always available to us, and we were always aware of the risk of driving after dark. We knew full well that for some reason there were people who felt our mere presence would poison their existence.

Lisa Page, a biracial woman, writes in an essay, "High Yellow White Trash," about how her white mother lost status as a white woman upon giving birth to Lisa in 1956. When in labor, she was placed in the white maternity section, but after giving birth to a biracial baby, she was immediately relegated to the "colored" section. Page notes that her mother was

"guilty by association; she was stained, privileged no more."
It wasn't until Page was an adolescent that her mother
revealed how much she had been hurt by this act.[3]

Although I rarely suffered from overt acts of racism, in my
childhood there was a palpable awareness of being black, of
being other. There was *this* world, a safe island of our people,
but there was also a wider world out there that affected our
reality in various ways and affected the way we saw ourselves, as well as, how we saw and treated each other.

Examples of this were evident in how adults and children
constantly named each other in terms of color, commenting
on the various shades of color and the meanings held within
those shades. "Get your black behind over here," or "Get out
of here, yellow girl." Or how one boy from our neighborhood, a dark, blue-black color, was nicknamed Spook. Or
those endless rounds of the dozens that seemed to always
begin with the phrase, "Your mama (is) so black she. . . ."

And then there was the rhyme that said it all:

> If you're black, get back
> If you're brown, stick around
> If you're yellow, you're mellow
> If you're white, you're all right.

Intuitively, we understood the truth of this rhyme and
learned to live within the system it described. Puberty's onset
turned attention toward the opposite sex, with constant rank-
ings of who was "cute" (and therefore desirable) and who
was not. Cute was generally shorthand for light-skinned with
"good" (read: not nappy) hair. For those with nappy ("bad")
hair, it became a civic duty to make yourself presentable by
straightening it.

The history of colorism, that chasm between light- and
dark-skinned African-Americans is a long and painful one.
During the period of African enslavement there were essentially two kinds of slaves: "house niggers" and "field niggers." House niggers were quite often the offspring of white
men and black women—owner and slave. Although they

were slaves, the biracial (a term not used then), lighter-skinned group enjoyed a moderately elevated status above the darker-skinned folks and was charged with helping keep the latter group in check. Throughout the history of Africans in the United States, there have always been individuals light enough to "pass" for white who disappeared into white society, cutting themselves off from black family, friends, and community forever.

As an adult, I've read enough memoirs and reflections and fictive depictions of black neighborhoods to understand we were part of a larger phenomenon. I've also learned that the light skin/dark skin thing is not unique to the African-American community, nor confined to the United States. Native American and Latino/a communities have similar colorism stories. Chinese American author Phoebe Eng reports that thousands of Asian American women buy themselves eye lifts each year to make their eyes rounder; it is the most frequently occurring plastic surgery among Asian women in America, nose buildups being second. In 1990, the American Society of Plastic and Reconstructive Surgery reported that over 39,000 reconstructive procedures were performed on Asians, making them more likely than any other people-of-color group to undergo the knife.

Although the United States has seemingly embraced its multicultural makeup, whiteness is still portrayed as the norm, the ultimate. bell hooks, in her 1992 book of essays *Black Looks*, writes, "That the field of representation remains a place of struggle is most evident when we critically examine contemporary representation of blackness and black people. I was painfully reminded of this fact recently when visiting friends on a once colonized black island. Their little girl is just reaching that stage of preadolescent life where we become obsessed with our image, with how we look, and how others see us. Her skin is dark. Her hair is chemically straightened. Not only is she fundamentally convinced that straightened hair is more beautiful than curly, kinky, natural hair, she believes that lighter skin makes one more worthy, more valuable in the eyes of others. Despite her parents' efforts to raise their children in an affirming black context, she has internalized white supremacist values and aesthetics. She has taken on a way of looking at and seeing the world that negates her value.

"Of course, this is not a new story. I could say the same for my nieces and nephews, and millions of black children here in the States. What struck me about this little girl was the depth of her pain and rage. She was angry, and yet her anger had no voice. And it struck me that for black people, the pain of learning that we cannot control our images—how we see ourselves or how we are seen—is so intense that it rends us. Often it leaves us ravaged by repressed rage, feeling weary, dispirited, and sometimes just plain old brokenhearted."[4]

The rage, weariness, and brokenheartedness that hooks speaks of are the soil in which the manifestations of internalized racist oppression grow. This is what feeds the destruction from within our communities, whether they are called ghettos, barrios, reservations, Little Hanoi's, or Chinatowns.

Internalizing inferiority messages affects one's ability to learn, to concentrate, and to be productive. Teacher Jane Elliot demonstrated this effectively with her classroom experiment "Brown Eyes, Blue Eyes." Many participants in antiracism workshops have watched on video the 1970 experiment carried out in Elliot's third-grade class of (all white) students in Riceville, Iowa. To teach them a lesson on discrimination, Elliot introduced a game in which students were divided by the color of their eyes—brown or blue. One day, the blue-eyed children were on top and given extra privileges and benefits based on their eye color. The next day the tables were turned and the brown-eyed children were the privileged set receiving all the benefits and encouragement. Almost immediately the effects of being categorized as "better" or "worse" people were evident. As the children internalized the messages, the ones on the bottom became aggressive, even violent, depressed, angry, and less capable in their schoolwork. A film of the experiment, "A Class Divided" was broadcast on the television show "Frontline."

In the 1987 book, *A Class Divided, Then and Now*, author

William Peters went back to get the story behind the story of Jane Elliot's experiment. He discovered that even Elliot was surprised at how rapidly the children latched onto their roles as superior and inferior people. She also had not expected their intellectual ability to be affected that quickly. Elliot said:

> If you know that no matter how hard you work, you will be called dumb because your eyes are the wrong color, will that make you want to try your hardest and do your best work? If you feel angry or sick or left out because of discrimination against you in school, are you going to want to go to school? Is it easy to keep your mind on your schoolwork when you know others are looking down on you because of the color of your eyes? . . . I wasn't pre-pared . . . for the degree of anger and rebellion expressed by *every child* at becoming a second-class citizen. (empha-sis mine)[5]

In the same way my Latina friends tell me of the humilia-tion they suffered in school because of their language and accent. Forbidden to speak Spanish, they were often labeled slow learners rather than given the language tools they need-ed in order to succeed. In high school, when it was time to begin deciding post-high school plans, they were often dis-couraged from pursuing higher education and directed instead toward trade schools. Like Elliot's third graders, self-doubt overshadowed any feeling of competency, but for peo-ple of color it often lingers for years, if not forever.

These experiences help cause our complicity in our own oppression. We essentially, often without being aware of it, agree with racism's assertion that we are less than. We begin to see our neighborhoods as bad, and ourselves as dumb, powerless, ugly . . . fill-in-the-blank. It must stop. What we believe on an individual level affects the outcome of our lives on cultural and institutional levels. How can our businesses grow if we believe they are inferior and don't patronize them? How can the entrepreneur gain credibility and secure funding if they are not used? How can our children excel if we don't think of them as capable? How can we dismantle racism if we believe we are inferior? How can we fulfill God's will for our lives if we believe we are fundamentally flawed aspects of creation?

Internalized racist oppression affects not only the way we see ourselves, but how we feel about our folkways, our ways of being. We have come to believe that our cultures (beliefs, practices, religious rituals, ways of dressing and speaking) are also inferior. In many places, white missionaries taught indigenous peoples that their expressions of spirituality, even when adapted to fit into the Christian context, were evil and had to be eliminated. In losing those parts of ourselves, we also lost the ability to recognize our cultural gifts. Instead, we became ashamed of them.

Phoebe Eng, in her book *Warrior Women*, writes about how even "good" stereotyping works against people-of-color groups. Stereotypes that cast Asians as the "model minorities" make it seem as if the bad things that happen to other people-of-color groups are their own fault. I heard a radio psychologist espouse this very line of thinking when, on her show, she pointed out how smart and successful Asian immigrants were because of how hard they worked. She didn't want to hear any more about how standardized tests were biased, because other groups obviously didn't do as well as whites and Asians because they weren't willing to work hard enough.

Eng asserts that the myth of the model minority "steers us away from the possibility that we might be average Americans struggling like everybody else, or that common inequities may exist across race lines among all Americans. Model minority myths support the belief that the racism ethnic groups complain about is the product of their own shortcomings. That is how this myth preserves status quo thinking." The myth also ignores information that questions the stereotypes. Census figures show that Asian American workers receive smaller economic rewards for their education than white workers, meaning Asian Americans need more education to maintain economic parity with whites. Asian

American students have the largest proportion of both the highest and lowest SAT scores, exploding the myth of super genius. Model minority myths conveniently point to higher average incomes of Asian households as compared to whites without also acknowledging that the average Asian family in America also has more members in the workforce. Of course, the myth completely ignores Asians who are living in poor communities across the country.

Yet, it is risky to initiate a conversation about internalized racist oppression among people of color. Many will deny that there even is such a thing. Part of this denial is the need to not air our dirty laundry in front of white folks—why give them more ammunition? Pretending we need to focus on our strengths and stop dwelling on the negative, or plain old denial that it affects us at all, are both tactics that help us avoid the subject. After all, we live in a "can do" society where the doors of opportunity are wide open for everyone. "Perhaps there's something wrong with you," one person of color says, "but certainly not me." Internalized racist oppression continues to serve racism by keeping us isolated from each other and inviting competition and hostility between people of color.

Resisting the system of racist oppression cannot be done authentically by ignoring the reality of the internalization process, particularly for people of color. We must take the risk. Our survival depends upon it.

2

The Decision to Be Whole

Some time later, Jesus went up to Jerusalem for a feast of the Jews. Now there is in Jerusalem near the Sheep Gate a pool, which in Aramaic is called Bethesda and which is surrounded by five covered colonnades. Here a great number of the disabled people used to lie— the blind, the lame, the paralyzed. One who was there had been an invalid for thirty-eight years. When Jesus saw him lying there and learned that he had been in this condition for a long time, he asked him, "Do you want to get well?"

"Sir," the invalid replied, "I have no one to help me into the pool when the water is stirred. While I am trying to get in, someone else goes down ahead of me." Then Jesus said to him, "Get up! Pick up your mat and walk." At once the man was cured; he picked up his mat and walked.
(John 5:1-8 NIV)

Like the man at Bethesda, those oppressed by racism often believe that our chance to be healed depends solely upon others lifting us up and taking us to the place of healing. It may seem we have not walked in so long that we have lost the use of our legs. The muscles are weak and atrophied and we lack the will to draw upon our own desire and our faith in the Creator to lift us up. We need to answer the question that Jesus asked, "Do you want to get well?" Until then, we will be blind to the possibilities of our lives and become paralyzed. Paralyzed individuals and families contribute to the paralysis of communities. While it is true that there is much life and beauty within our communities, the fact remains that there is sickness that needs to be acknowledged and then made well.

Earlier struggles for survival against overt, life threatening racism left little time to dwell upon ourselves as individuals. The urgency of the situation directed energy and resources toward changing the manifestations of racism that destroyed our bodies. The time has come to give equal attention to the damage racism has done to our psyches and souls.

One thing that legalized segregation forced upon people of color was the necessity to depend upon God and each other for survival. Throughout the eras of colonialism, slavery, reconstruction, and various movements for peace and freedom, our rich religious traditions have sustained us and in the words of the African-American spiritual, "made a way out of no way." Our ancestors understood the sustaining power of deep faith, a willingness to let mystery be mystery coupled with the strength to move forward. Rather than understand religion as an oppressive force for folks who could not think for themselves, they understood to the very marrow of their bones the liberating force of the gospel. Much of that faith has been handed down to us and retained, yet much needs to be rediscovered. Although not unscathed by racism, the church has been a sanctuary for people of color. Civil right movements have their roots in the church, as people have understood God's demand for justice for the oppressed. Freedom songs spring directly from African-American spirituals, and the biblical story of the Exodus inspired many.

Generations of people of color in this country grew up in tightly knit, segregated communities where people knew one another and stood up for one another. Those working toward desegregation thought once achieved, it would bring about the melting pot so many dreamed of. Instead, desegregation did other things, unexpected things. It brought an end to neighborhood schools. Affirmative action lifted people out of poverty and working class status into the middle class. People of color were able to move into areas where they had formerly been denied access. These were the fruits of hard-won battles, but as the best and brightest moved up and out, poor neighborhoods of color were destabilized. It looks slightly different in each community, but there are similarities. A growing sense of shame and the incurring struggle to hide poverty increased stress and led people to look for any means possible to escape. Money and things came to be seen as more important than people and relationships.

Middle class and wealthy folks of color who are in touch with reality and honest will tell you that it does not matter how much money they have, there is still the stigma of their color to tell them what their "place" in life is. People who left their communities find themselves without roots. Those left behind lose political power and access, and in so doing, become apathetic. They are not paid attention to, so they don't vote; they don't vote, so they are not paid attention to. Poor neighborhoods struggle without role models. The balance of strengths and struggles that formerly worked together fall out of kilter. When the people with money leave, there is less money left to circulate. Businesses and services leave so they can survive.

Desegregation of the schools took away the concept of neighborhood schools in many areas. It became difficult for parents to be involved in schools that were across town, participation in after-school programs decreased, and funding for busing took money away for other needs schools have. Many of our city schools across the country have or are facing huge deficits that force them to have high teacher turnover, resulting in a surplus of young, inexperienced teachers, outdated and insufficient numbers of textbooks, and buildings that are falling apart around the children's heads. It does not foster a desire to learn and succeed.

As the spiral circles downward, people begin to look for ways to cope with the added stresses of their lives. It becomes a living example of the "broken window" theory: if a broken window in a building on an otherwise well cared for block is not repaired, it invites another broken window, and another. Trash and a general sense of disrepair follow until the block is completely broken down. In the abandoned neighborhoods and in the middle- and upper-class neighborhoods where the dream does not quite match the reality, substance abuse, violence, and other crimes quickly follow. It becomes easy to believe that we cannot be "made well."

All of our work on behalf of antiracism will mean nothing if we do not take care of ourselves emotionally, psychologically, and spiritually. The woundedness is deep, but healing is available. We must still believe this and move toward healing ourselves in order to sustain the hard work of antiracism.

Our own wholeness begins with making a personal decision

The language of evangelism fosters our understanding of "making a personal decision." We understand that although we live and move within community and are called to the creation of a just society, we still must say yes to God. It is an act of affirmation of our total dependence upon God, and our promise to give our will over to God. It is the beginning of our wholeness. With that act, we are brought back into oneness of purpose with creation and the Creator.

Part of our wholeness is understanding ourselves as part of creation that God has blessed and declared good. "Do you not know that you are the Lord's temple?" Paul asked. Peter learned never to declare anything unclean which the Lord has called clean. Wholeness is far beyond simply having good self-esteem; it is part of our calling to recognize the wonder of all creation, including our darker skinned selves.

We can begin by remembering and honoring our own traditions. For many of us, it will take some research to learn about our family histories and heritage. Because of the ongoing struggle to include all people's history in school curriculums, it will mean doing much of the research ourselves and then passing on the information to others. In doing so, we should not forget our living resources, our elders. We can travel back to the places we came from and research our family trees. We must take care of our minds, and make education a priority, recognizing that book learning is not the most important learning, but in order to get ahead, we must be prepared. Our children drop out of school too often. As adults we must work to make the educational system relevant to their experiences.

Taking care of our bodies

The rapid pace of life today takes its toll on our bodies and we forget the common sense methods we all know that help keep them healthy. The way our bodies feel has an impact on our minds so we need to pay attention to them. We need to eat healthy foods—more fruits and vegetables, less processed foods, less meat. We must learn how to cook our traditional foods in new ways when necessary that cut down on fat and salt. We need to tell ourselves and each other to get enough rest and exercise. We should get out of the cities and back to the land so we can touch the earth, touch water. Some of our children have never been out of the cities they were born in. We need to talk about our dreams and aspirations, acknowledging their importance. As we do this, we should write down the things we learn about ourselves.

Drug addiction is rampant in our communities. Every church should sponsor or in some way support Alcoholics Anonymous and Narcotics Anonymous meetings, as well as support groups that address other needs such as people living with AIDS and survivors of domestic and sexual abuse. Make it known that the church is a place for hurting people. Jesus noted that it is the sick that need a doctor, not the well. Too often our churches become sanctuaries for the "holier than thou," rather than an emergency room for the critically wounded. When people come for these healing ministries, they should not be made to feel that they are unwelcome intruders, but a part of the community that the church is called to minister to. We can also be open to being ministered to *by* those struggling with addiction.

Taking care of our children

Our children are important enough to fight for. First of all, we must tell them every day that they are beautiful, smart, and capable, God's own child. At the same time, we need to tell them about the realities of racism and prepare them for a racist society. Create places for them to feel their beauty, intelligence, and capability. Give them the time and the places to learn their dances, their art, and their music.

Showing up at school is of prime importance. Parents and guardians can let teachers and administrators know that we are concerned about our children's education by being a visible presence at school. It is vital for us to be partners in our children's education, to be there in order to support their teachers, and to be watchdogs if necessary. For many of us this is difficult. Transportation, language barriers, and work schedules may make it nearly impossible to show up at school. There are ways for the church community to be involved. Members can help visit schools. Pastors and other leaders can visit schools in their church's neighborhoods and other schools attended by their members. In my own congregation, an after-school tutoring program started by one of our members opened the door to partnering with the public school system. This program does several things: provides outreach to children and their parents in the community, strengthens the children academically, provides a setting for the building of intergenerational relationships, gives teenagers work experience, and gives the children precious one-on-one interaction with an adult on a regular basis.

Concentrate and focus your energy on your neighborhood. Rather than concentrating on moving kids around to achieve racial balance, work at making schools places where families want to send their children. Work on changing the way schools are funded so that the quality of a school doesn't rely on the strength of the tax base in the city.

Talk and pray and plan what your congregation is called to do to minister to children. Promote and support efforts to foster and adopt children. County social service agencies are bursting at the seams with children of color who need families.

Taking care of our communities—what individuals and families can do

Ritual is an important part of the lives of communities of faith. It can be used to affirm our identity in Christ and our place within the community. Baptism and communion are two of our most common rituals. These two in particular bind us to our present communities and to centuries of Christians who have gone before. They bind us to the very person of Christ.

Individual rituals can include regular prayer and meditation. Create a special place, even if it's only a corner in a room. Determine your spiritual sensibility. For some it will be reading a book of daily meditations along with Scripture readings, while others will journal or draw. Let your senses become involved: light a candle as a visible reminder of the presence of the Holy Spirit, let the scent of herbs or flowers remind you of God's goodness. Whatever your skill or gift is, whether cooking, gardening, or mentoring, see these acts as prayers as well, living sacrificial acts.

Family rituals can include making a point of eating together, discussing the best and worst thing each day, or celebrating birthdays and other milestones in unique ways. Gathering regularly as an extended family is a ritual many families are returning to, some have never left. Remember many of us are single, and/or no longer near our extended families. Congregations can be an important part of building new family connections for all of our members.

Congregational rituals can include the traditional ones

like child blessing ceremonies, the gift of a Bible, or com-memoration when an individual or a family moves away. We can also come together to celebrate important events in our cultural histories, bringing that part of our experience into our faith expressions. Congregations should embrace any-thing that says, "You are a precious creation of God, God val-ues you and we value you."

Jesus asked the man at the pool if he wanted to be healed. The man skirted around the question because he was certain he needed the actions of others to bring about his healing. When this did not happen, time after time, he gave up. However, at Jesus' command, he was able to walk. Another time, Jesus healed a different person: a woman bleeding for many years and outcast from the community because of her uncleanliness. In her case, she reached out to touch Jesus in one last bold attempt to make herself well. Jesus called her "daughter," and said her faith had made her clean. In the same way, Jesus urges all who suffer to reach out in faith and grab hold of their healing.

3

Of Systems and Powers

Here is my servant, whom I uphold,
*   my chosen one in whom I delight;*
I will put my Spirit on him and he will bring justice to the nations.
He will not shout or cry out, or raise his voice in the streets.
A bruised reed he will not break, and a smoldering wick he will not
snuff out. In faithfulness he will bring forth justice; he will not fal-
ter or be discouraged till he establishes justice on earth. . . .
This is what the Lord God says:
"I, the Lord, have called you in righteousness; I will take hold of
your hand. I will keep you and will make you to be a covenant for
the people and a light for the Gentiles, to open eyes that are blind,
to free captives from prison and to release from the dungeon those
who sit in darkness.
I am the Lord; that is my name!
I will not give my glory to another or my praise to idols. See, the
former things have taken place, and new things I declare; before they
spring into being I announce them to you."
(Isaiah 42:1-8 NIV)

Why should people of color care about systems in our struggle for liberation?

The iceberg that we introduced as a metaphor for racism is multileveled and three dimensional. The three dimensions, or manifestations of racism that we talk about are individual, cultural, and institutional, and each of the three are realized at every level of the iceberg. At the tip, the Oppressive Power of racism is painfully evident and is often the only visible part. White Power, racism's power to provide power and privilege to white people lies in the middle, and Identity Power, racism's attempt to tell white people and people of color who they are, is at the base level.

The internalization of racist oppression is perhaps felt most deeply and seen most obviously in its individual manifestations: the self-hatred and doubting of our abilities and the abilities of those that look most like us. It is in the individual where it is easiest to see the damage racism does to people of color; this is what makes most people believe that working against racism means changing the hearts of the people doing the hurting and "fixing" the people who have been hurt. And so we have diversity training and multicultural festivals and choir exchanges and the like, and racism rolls along merrily, changing its shape to adapt to the changes put in place by good people who want to see racism end.

In our work, we believe that it is institutions that must be changed. Individuals must interact with institutions, and so there is a relationship, a point of connection between their corresponding sides of the iceberg, and people often find it difficult to bridge the perceived gap between the two sides. When we think of institutions, we think of large, impersonal entities that by their very design are difficult to change. Most of us are not used to thinking about institutions, yet we interact with them all the time. To combat racism, clear connections need to be made between the individual experiences of racism and its effects, and that individual's interactions with institutions that have the power to shape our lives. No one is born a racist or a victim. Instead, individual racists and individual victims are systematically created. It is important to understand, then, the system.

The Bible uses the language of systems. Paul writes that we wrestle not against flesh and blood, but against the powers and principalities—the systems. Faith communities have long looked to the Scriptures for comfort, and to Jesus as one who gives strength and courage to persevere through the pain of oppression. It is also Jesus who empowers the oppressed to seek their liberation. To all believers, Jesus calls for active resistance against all oppression. We can see in the Gospel accounts Jesus teaching and leading an active resistance against the traditions of his times that embodied the oppressive structures. Rather than passive pacifism, the gospel demands active social transformation. Jesus ministered to the "crowd": the social outcasts, the poor, the blind and the lame, women and children, and Gentiles. He specifically sought out those outside the sphere of dominance and power. But he came for all.

In his descriptions of the kingdom, Jesus spoke a language that all could hear and understand, with images of home and common work. "To what shall we compare the kingdom of heaven?" To a man who sowed good seed in his field, a mustard seed, or yeast a woman mixes with flour. With these images, Jesus is saying that the kingdom of heaven is what you least expect. Jesus' parables of the kingdom do not exclude or reject the powerless. Instead, the powerless are at the very center of the image. Jesus touched and was touched by the untouchable and commanded his followers to do the same. He was outrageous in his actions, using spit (unclean) to heal blindness and calling "daughter" a woman separated from the holy community by a continuous issue of blood. As he brought those outcast from the margins to the center, he restored their humanity *in their own eyes.* Jesus did not dispense compassion on the downtrodden simply to relieve their individual suffering, but to announce the reign of God. The message undergirding these actions was always the same: the kingdom is for all who will come, and all have equal status before the Lord.

After Jesus' death and resurrection, one of the most tension-provoking problems for the early church was the same one Jesus dealt with. Who is to be included? Who may enter? Who is really human? Who has the power and authority to decide the fate and position of every one else? It is still our issue today, with many variations on the same theme. Why does it seem resolving this problem once and for all is out of our grasp? "For our struggle is not against flesh and blood, but against the . . . powers of this dark world and against the spiritual forces of evil in the heavenly realms" (Eph. 6:12).

Biblical scholar Walter Wink has written extensively on what the apostle Paul identifies as our struggle, completing a series of books on the powers: *Naming the Powers*, *Unmasking the Powers*, and *Engaging the Powers*. According to Wink, any attempt to face the problem of evil in society from a New Testament perspective must include an understanding of the "principalities and powers" that Paul speaks of. Wink acknowledges that most people regard the powers as either mere superstition, or simply institutions, structures, and systems. That institutions have an actual spiritual ethos is a notion our modern, materially oriented society finds difficult to grasp, but this has not always been the case. Ancient and traditional worldviews have long understood that the physical and spiritual worlds are entities not completely separate from one another.

At its most simplistic, Wink describes the powers as the spirituality of systems and structures that have betrayed their divine vocations. Wink uses the expression "Domination System" to describe a system of powers that have become integrated around idolatrous values. The domination system has forgotten who God is, and made itself out to be God. It has made itself the entity that is to be served. Thus, the original intent of institutions and systems as created by God were good, but the powers are now fallen and the powers must be redeemed.

Within the framework of a domination system, racism serves the system by creating people who have either internalized superiority or inferiority based on skin color. The system keeps both classes locked into a predictable pattern of actions and reactions. *Individuals* moving themselves out of the system do not stop the actions and reactions, they are merely replaced. To stop the racism machine, a concerted action by critical masses of people whose intent is to dismantle the system is necessary. The task calls for people working in solidarity with one another: white people and people of color, racists and victims.

The system of racism cannot be overpowered by individuals working singly. Individual will and action cannot overcome the powers. Individuals do need to be aware of the personal cost racism exacts and its cost on society and creation. Individuals need to make the decision to be working against racism and are responsible for changing their own behavior and how they participate in the system. But a big picture focus is still needed. The presence of racism in our day-to-day lives is informed by the policies, procedures, missions, and behaviors of the institutions we interact with.

Looking at the racism iceberg
Oppressive Power

If nothing else is known about racism, the oppressive power of racism is generally what people think of first. Racism's oppressive power is in the acts of racism that hurt and kill people of color: the slavery of Africans, the colonization of what has come to be called the Americas, the systematic genocide of Native peoples, and the internment of Japanese Americans. These visible acts of oppression are part of a larger system that says it is okay to do this because people of color are not even human. Although less visible in modern times, it is still seen today through hate crimes and various forms of harassment. People of color understand that they are not a part of "the American dream."

One result of this continued reality is the double consciousness many people of color experience because we must decide, day by day, moment by moment, where we will be physically safe. Even when a place has been determined to be safe, at any moment the rug may be pulled from underneath. There is never an opportunity, it seems, to stop being black or brown or red, and just be. Last summer a large group of youth from our congregation attended our denomination's youth conference, a biennial event that attracts several thousand youth, mostly white, from across the country. Our group of twenty kids was mostly African-American, but included biracial and white youth. Everything seemed to go pretty well for the most part, except the day when one of our boys was stopped on the street in front of the convention center and frisked by the police. Dozens of white teenagers were milling about and he was not causing a disturbance, yet he was given a not so subtle message of "you don't belong here."

Another member of our congregation, a woman, has a similar story. She is legally blind and uses a guide dog. While recently traveling with friends from church to a meeting several hours away, they stopped at a fast-food restaurant for a meal in an all white area. All three women are middle-aged African-Americans. Upon entering the restaurant, my friend was informed pets were not allowed. The women explained that the dog was not a pet, but a working guide dog that allowed her owner to get around safely and that the dog was properly trained and registered. The restaurant employees, including the manager, were not moved. Eventually the sheriff was called and the women left, fearful, angered, and humiliated. Again, the message "you don't belong here" rang out loud and clear. This was not the 1940s South, but the Midwest in the late 1990s.

In both of these cases, people may argue that the St. Louis cop and the fast-food cashier were acting upon individual impulses and their actions cannot fairly be used as examples of racism at work. Perhaps they had a bad day, or they were mean people, or they misunderstood or misused the policies of the institution. However, in each instance, the people involved were acting on behalf of the institutions they worked for. Messages from the institution give tacit approval to the racist actions of individuals.

White Power

The core of the racism iceberg we have labeled White Power; it is where racism's purpose resides because racism is not really about hurting people of color, it is about giving privilege and power to white people. Within the system of racism, white people are superior. The things that happen at the tip of the iceberg, the incidents of oppressive power, happen because of this core. This is where our institutions have fallen away from their divine purpose, and in Wink's terms, the powers are fallen. As white people are provided power and privilege based solely on white skin and people of color are given less power and less privilege, the internalization process germinates.

For example, the common experience of people of color, particularly African-American men, not being able to hail a taxi is felt most keenly in the moment of the individual act (the driver) toward another individual (the person needing a ride). Supporting the driver's individual act is an institutional (taxi company) policy, whether written or unwritten, formal or informal, understanding that there are certain people "we" do not have to pick up and certain areas "we" do not have to drive in. The decision not to pick the man up is an individual one, but it is the institution that is part of a larger system (transportation) that gives permission for the decision to be made.

In Cleveland, the city where I live, the baseball team's mascot is a caricature of a Native American and has been declared offensive by Native Americans. Many individuals choose to buy merchandise portraying the logo; in fact it has been one of the most popular logos in the league. Common rebuttals to the mascot protestors include comments such as "it's not an insult, it's meant to be a tribute," "it's not that big a deal, go protest something important," and "I can wear whatever I want." Because the people who favor the offensive mascot reason that it is their individual right to purchase and wear whatever they like, the movement to change the mascot and logo is only political correctness taken too far.

At first glance it seems as if the whole matter concerns

individual preferences. No one is being forced to wear the logo, some people enjoy it and others don't. But, the fact remains that the white institution gets to decide what the representation of Native Americans shall be, gets to decide the meaning of the representation, and gets the economic benefits from selling merchandise the representation appears on. These institutional decisions would not be so easily made were it not for the systemic reality of how Native Americans have been viewed and treated on their own land since the European invasion in the 1400s. The system of racism says that what white people want to wear is more important than the dignity of people of color. The protests against offensive representations are brushed off. Comments of parents who report their children being humiliated in school by students who come up and chant "war whoops," who pull their hair, and mock their culture are ignored. It is the Native children and their parents who end up being labeled as too sensitive, not playing with the team or fitting in. If they retaliate, they are then labeled as violent and the stereotype of violent savage is perpetuated. Some Native Americans have even been told to go back where they came from! The issue is far from settled and goes beyond a few professional teams. An article in the Summer 1999 issue of *Native Peoples* reports that in the United States nearly 2,000 school athletic programs continue to use Native American images as their mascots and logos.

Identity Power

The most damaging level of racism is at the iceberg's base. It is racism claiming the power to tell people of color and white people who they are. God has already named each of us, down to the very hairs upon our heads. Racism attempts to usurp God's authority. It is at the Identity Power level that racism begins to shape us, and tells us what to think and what to feel about ourselves.

Among children and youth of color (and even some adults) there is a phenomenon known as "acting white," and it is generally meant as an insult. "Acting white" includes, among other things, being studious, getting good grades, and enunciating clearly and speaking "proper" English. There are "white" sports and "white" clubs to join, "white" music and "white" clothes. I don't think this is simply a matter of preferences, that whites and people of color just happen to prefer different things based on their color and culture and these preferences happen to always fall along particular lines. It seems more a matter of being assigned one's place in the system and then "choosing" to fit within the boundaries of the stereotype that purport to define one's reality.

The subtext of the acting white accusation is this: "You are not white and you never will be. You will never be accepted into that privileged existence, no matter how smart you are, how properly you speak, or how well you play hockey. So don't even try." The converse, of course, is putting on a show about how much we don't want to be white and don't care about "white" values and so we don't study, don't participate in any activities, and so on. Part of it is protecting ourselves from inevitable rejection by pretending we don't care. The more insidious part is believing that we are just not good enough, we are just not capable.

The belief goes beyond what individuals think of themselves. It affects how we view others that look like us and in turn how we deal with them: what stores we patronize, what books we read, what neighborhoods we try to move into, and how we treat our children. We are never able to see ourselves as we really are, our view is always mediated through the lens of racism. This is but the beginning of the damaging effects of racism's identity shaping power over people of color.

In 1988 the *New York Times* featured a story about African-American residents in a New Jersey neighborhood resisting attempts to rename their street after Dr. Martin Luther King because it would signal to people reading the phone book that it was a black neighborhood. They said such knowledge would stigmatize the area. This is the mark of internalized racist oppression, when your very identification as an individual or as part of a group becomes a stigma. Identities, given to us by God, should not be something we seek to overcome or something we seek to hide.

As individuals committed to the task of dismantling racism, we must learn to speak the language and understand the role of principalities and powers. Jesus' new social order called for the turning inside out of the expectations of those at the top *and* those at the bottom. We are called to do no less with our expectations.

4

Journey Toward Destruction: colonization of the mind

And a woman was there who had been subject to bleeding for twelve years. She had suffered a great deal under the care of may doctors and had spent all she had, yet instead of getting better she grew worse. When she heard about Jesus, she came up behind him in the crowd and touched his cloak because she thought, "If I just touch his clothes, I will be healed."
(Mark 5:25-28 NIV)

Systemic powers: a view from the Bible
I'm not quite sure if I should go out today, but I heard Jesus was in town. If people recognize me I could be stoned to death. I'm tired of being viewed as unclean, the outsider. Was it my fault I fell ill twelve years ago? I've done everything in my power to find healing but I am still seen as unclean. When I start to feel sorry for myself

I think of the others like me who are seen as unclean. Like me, many of them did not have a choice. I can't understand it but yet I know if I go out and touch others they too will become unclean. My uncleanness has kept me apart from so many things in the community. I long to be seen as a human being with the same feelings as others. Instead I am treated with disregard and contempt.

What if I was to view myself as clean? Maybe people wouldn't recognize me. I bet there will be many people there today. The word is out that Jesus heals the unclean and I am sure many like me will go seeking wholeness. I need to have faith that I can do this. Maybe I really do need to think of myself as clean. I will venture into the community and seek out Jesus, the one who has power to make clean that which is unclean. I know that if I could just touch his robe that will be all I need. I better get ready to go so that I will not miss his visit to our village.

I must first begin to believe that I myself can be clean.

I have often wondered what the woman hemorrhaging for twelve years in Mark 5 was thinking just before she ventured out of her home in hopes of encountering Jesus. I do know that in order for anyone to overcome their internalized oppression they must view themselves as a worthy human being. Those oppressed must be able to see themselves as someone no longer held in the bondage of the oppression.

I believe there is a correlation between systemic internalized racist oppression and the internalization of uncleanness of those viewed as unclean in the Old and New Testament. This correlation may help us uncover the systemic realities of both systems. Sometimes being able to view our society and its institutions and systems systemically is very difficult, especially by most white people of the United States. This stems from two realities, the first being the individualistic culture that is so pervasive in the United States. The second reality is if you are part of the group reaping the benefits and privileges of a system, you are socialized not to see it.

The purification system, during the time of Jesus, became a system that served the elite of the temple. In its social construct, purification served the few and oppressed the many. It became a very lucrative business for a small minority, while most of the population were taxed and spent their money for sacrifices. A system that was meant for the people, became a system of oppression.

Among scholars, there is much speculation about why the purification system was first put in place. Some believe it was God's way of protecting the Israelites and setting them apart as a distinct people. The purification system became a system of classification of persons, places, times, and things. Here we will focus on the classification of people. A system whose original intent may have been to protect a people and create a distinctive peoplehood, soon became an elaborate system of who's in and who's out.

The purification system became a social construct to determine whether persons were "pure" or "polluted." It served as a way to establish and maintain group identity, ultimately having the power to include or exclude. Like racism, the purification system decided who was "normal" or "whole." Some of the similarities between the purification system and racism have to do with the classification of people, hierarchy, the setting of norms and standards, and a system viewed as fact by the group administrating the system within their society. The three elements that ultimately turned the cultural practice of purification into a systemic oppressive power were economics, political power, and a religious ideology to support the system. As Marcus Borg said "Ordinary people had no power over the shape or direction of society."[1] These same elements have made systemic racism so oppressive in our own time.

And so this woman, who had been hemorrhaging for twelve years, was labeled "unclean" by her own system. After twelve years of being viewed as such by society, it must have begun to have a great impact on her as a person and specifically what she was able to do within her own community. When this happens, it is no longer a matter of a person's individual experiences, but an experience lived within a societal context and systemic reality. Where this woman could go, who she could interact with, and how she lived her life daily was no longer dictated by individual will, but by the political will of the community. How the woman viewed herself was not only from an individual point of view but also from the view of her society. In many ways, the purification laws classified people into a social construct of "unclean." Racism also classifies people into the social construct of race. Racism has been ingrained into the social fabric of our society and with racism comes concrete standards and norms out of which we, as a society, operate.

The woman who was hemorrhaging had allowed those in power to name the problem, that she was unclean. She also, for twelve years, went along with the norms and standards of her society, a society that dictated her place. She may have come to believe that she deserved her assigned place on the margins and was not entitled to full participation within the community. The internalization of such beliefs has grave impact not just on individuals, but on groups of people.

As people of color we can learn a great deal about the courage it takes to look at our identities from the model of the bleeding woman. One specific lesson is that we need to have faith in ourselves. I find it remarkable that in this story it does not mention that Jesus said she had to have faith in him. Rather, Jesus said, "Your faith has made you well." We also must be willing to have faith enough in God, that God will be there, when we are ready to step counter to what society is dictating. We are speaking about a person's inner strength. The ability to go counter against such powers in society takes tremendous courage and faith to believe that we are able.

When we work against systemic oppressive powers, like what the purification practice became in time, and racism, it can appear to be overwhelming. If the woman had never ventured out to touch Jesus because of the hopelessness of her situation, we would probably understand. But the transformative nature of this very story is that God's healing power did not become contaminated by her touch, in fact, the opposite happened. God's healing power transformed what was unclean, making her clean. This is such a powerful image for people of color as we work on dismantling internalized racist oppression on a systemic level. We too can be transformed to "whole" and "well" people.

All people groups need to be valued as human beings created in the image of God. Each people group brings a worldview that is a contribution to the body of Christ. In January 2000 I attended a World Christian Indigenous Gathering in Australia. During the opening ceremony, everyone was asked to dress in traditional attire. I am Mexic-Amerindian, and I had brought with me a traditional Mexican blouse, however, I was hesitant to wear it because it was fashioned after our colonizers' dress, Spain. As I talked with others about my hesitation, they knew what I was talking about and encouraged me to look deeper into my ancestry. At the next gathering, I will come in traditional dress to reflect my indigenous heritage. The awareness and the encouragement to embrace who I really am and where I come from has been such a tremendous journey.

Besides the individual human need to feel acceptance, we also need acceptance as a people. At the gathering in Australia, I was asked to share a little about who I am. As I said I was a descendant of the great Aztec Nation, a roar of affirmation with yells, drums, and cries rang throughout the auditorium. That was the first time in my entire life I heard such affirmation for my ancestry. It was a spiritual transformation.

We, as people of color, must retain who we are. If institutions and systems are to change we will need other worldviews to create alternative institutions and systems that are not founded on dominance and/or hierarchy. I believe people of color, with their varied worldviews, may hold a piece of the puzzle in helping transform the church to be inclusive, and also antiracist.

One of the questions that was asked at the indigenous gathering was, "If you are created in God's image, is not your culture a gift to the larger Christian community? What do you bring as an offering to God?" But the problem with most people of color is that we don't know what we bring because we do not know who we are, nor do we see ourselves as a gift. Internalized racist oppression's main goal is to have people of color participate in maintaining racism. To do this, internalized oppression defines people of color as second-class citizens with a sense of not having anything to contribute to our society. Whether in secular society or the church, we continue to be the colonized internally.

Continuing on, I will share with you ways that we allow ourselves to be destroyed within institutions and systems in the United States. My hope is not to place blame, but to find truth and ways to begin to liberate ourselves to be who God created us to be in this world. I believe each culture has something to contribute to the kingdom of God equally; God was in every culture before Europeans ever came to this continent. There is no superior way to serve or worship God in God's eyes. The ancient Aztec philosopher once asked, "How best is truth spoken?" Prince Tecayechuatzin answered, "Only flower and song can express truth." May what I share with you become a song within your soul to resist what oppresses you as you begin to write your own song of liberation.

Myths and lies

To talk about internalized racist oppression I will be using the interconnected words "institutions" and "systems," institutions being part of a larger system. For example, elementary schools, universities, and middle schools are institutions within the larger system known as the educational system. It is important that we understand the connection of institutions and systems in order to help us understand how we are socialized. Most of our socialization, on a systemic level, happens through institutions in our society. The "unclean" woman discussed before was probably socialized into the purification system through her family and the temple. Both family and the temple, or church, are very powerful institutions even today.

Internalized racist oppression has a spiraling affect on people. Using the image of a spiral helps us see how certain elements of internalized racist oppression repeat themselves upon previous experiences. I will limit my illustration of the spiral to institutions and systems, but the spiral image can also be used on an individual and community level.

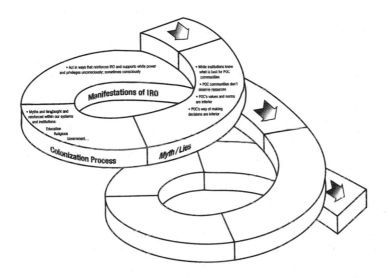

When people internalize oppression many things take place and the spiral starts with three segments which, over time, repeat themselves within many historical settings: the slave trade, colonization of First Nations peoples, Mexicans, Hawaiians, and Puerto Ricans, and manifestations like our anti-immigration policies. The first segment of the spiral is the myths and lies we have accepted as truth, specifically that: 1. White institutions should name the problem and know what is best for people of color communities, 2. people of color do not deserve resources for their communities and/or themselves, 3. people of color's values and norms are inferior, and 4. people of color's way of making decisions are inferior.[2] These are not the only myths or lies, but are some of the most destructive to us as people of color on a systemic level. These four myths are quite powerful because they are interconnected, like a spiderweb. When you act on one of these myths/lies you are most likely acting on one or two of the others.

Why, for example, would we believe that white people know what is best for us? The constant reinforcement of this myth can be found in almost every institution in the United States. The very premise of colonization is to hold up one group as superior. When we are at a place where we are able to recognize the myth, we must then remember our own cultural traditions. In the Mexic-Amerindian culture, life experiences and wisdom are valued above intellectual or analytical empirical knowledge. When Mexic-Amerindians make decisions based on wisdom, life experiences, and our own spiritual understandings, we are often confronted by questions from the dominant culture as to why we made a certain decision. It is not viewed as a good decision unless we can back it up with facts. When we run into these critiques over and over again, we too begin to believe what the dominant culture is telling us. We believe that unless we are able to back our decisions with facts and analytical reasoning, we are not making good decisions.

But this is not the way it should be. We need to feel confident and okay about decisions we make for our communities and ourselves. We must value our worldview and ways in which decisions are made within our own cultural understanding. Being able to accept who we are is interconnected with the whole idea of who sets standards and decides what is "normal," an issue I will address later.

Colonization process

The myths and lies feeding internalized racist oppression are reinforced by the dominant culture through socialization. Institutions we have been taught to trust, like the educational and health systems or church and government agencies, impress the myths and lies on our minds. This information affects us on several levels: our personal well-being, our communities, our culture, and how we interact and are treated within institutions and systems. Through the teaching and socialization of these myths and lies we, as a people, begin to believe what we have heard and have systemically been taught about ourselves, so begins the colonizing of our minds.

The type of power these messages have on us begins early in life. By age three, 90 percent of who we are is already set. This is not to say that change cannot and does not happen, but the foundation has been laid. So the messages we receive early in our lives have tremendous impact in the formation of who we are as individuals and in turn, how we interact within our communities.

The most effective way to colonize people is to have them internalize the ideology of the dominant culture. If the oppressors are successful in colonizing minds, then their overt work of colonization is over and the colonized continue to perpetuate the cycle of oppression within their own communities. I have experienced this even in my own life. As a Mexic-Amerindian I was raised to believe light skin was better. If you could identify as Spanish or French you were better off, and if you were dark-skinned, too bad for you. I remember my paternal grandmother, who was obsessed with light skin, telling me it was a shame I looked "Indio." I am not here to judge my grandmother, nor do I blame her because she was a product, like you and I, of a racist society.

Playing into our internalized racist oppression is the rewards given to people of color who support the myths. For supporting white supremacy and power, they are made to feel like they are given a piece of the power and privilege, and in turn, the system punishes those who overtly resist. In the same way, we see in the story of the woman bleeding, the response Jesus got as he allowed his power to be released to an unclean woman. He also went to Jarius' house and touched Jarius' dead daughter and brought her to life. His deed did not go unnoticed by the Pharisees; in fact, they were angered by his disregard for the tradition. They wanted him dead. He was a threat because he was not complying with the status quo of the purification tradition. In a later chapter, I will speak more about how the system responds when people of color resist oppression.

Manifestations of internalized racist oppression

Intragroup hostility

Institutionally, people of color start to reinforce what we have been taught against ourselves and our own people. Often when I am on the Texas-Mexico border I get angry when I see Mexican-Americans working as border patrol. But how can I be angry? These men and women are living out what they have been taught. I have often heard Mexicans say that Mexican-American border patrol are more abusive than the "Anglo" border patrol. Our belief that we are inferior is especially obvious by how we treat our own people and how we reinforce the colonization of our mind. This is the phase, in the downward spiral of destruction, where we no longer have to wait for the dominant culture to kill us. We are killing ourselves.

Amnesia

We forget where we came from and who we are as a people. Sometimes we do this out of self-preservation because of the systemic racism in the United States. It becomes very difficult at times to be able to free oneself from the systemic reality of racism. In the last year, when I have been on the Mexican side of the border, the racism that is encountered in the United States by Mexican nationals is so clear. When they relay story after story of the racism they encounter, they are very clear as to how they experience the racism. I believe their clarity has to do with the fact that they are coming into the systemic racism of this country instead of being born into it like many of us. The very nature of an oppressive system is to envelop both the oppressed and the oppressor so that the oppressive system is kept in place and not even noticed.

When the downward spiral is complete, we experience the myths and lies in different arenas of our lives, and the

cycle begins again. One experience on top of another reinforces what we have been taught to believe about ourselves.
It's as though we forget who we are, and this amnesia allows
us to again get caught in the cycle. Much like the "battered
woman syndrome," we forget what has just happened to us,
believing that it won't happen again. Just as a battered
woman knows her place within her family and society, and
the "unclean" of the purification system in biblical times, we
no longer have to be told what our place is and who we are,
we know.

The hemorrhaging woman's very act of coming into town
and mingling with the group took great inner strength. Her
ability to see herself outside of society's prescribed norms
took incredible courage. She took this step in order to live
fully the life God intended. For us, as people of color in the
United States, it will take that same kind of strength to see
ourselves outside of a racist society's prescribed norms. And
we must be willing not to forget what has happened in order
to escape the cycle.

Summary

Like the woman with the issue of blood, I too want to be
whole. I know the same transformative power God has
wielded in my life as an individual is possible on a systemic
level. I dream of what a whole society might look like, and at
times get glimpses of my dream. I believe an antiracist world
is part of God's kingdom: a place where we will all be loved
and the only power that will be administered will be through
God's power of unconditional love for all of creation. We can
face the demon of internalized racist oppression and I believe
we can journey toward wholeness as a people of God.

5

Journey Toward Wholeness: decoloniza-tion of the mind

*Immediately her bleeding stopped and she felt in her body that she
was freed from her suffering.*
*At once Jesus realized that power had gone out from him. He turned
around in the crowd and asked, "Who touched my clothes?"*
*"You see the people crowding against you," his disciples answered,
"and yet you can ask, 'Who touched me?'"*
But Jesus kept looking around to see who had done it.
(Mark 5:28-32 NIV)

Once we are able to visualize how internalized racist oppression works, we are then able to think about how we journey
toward wholeness. We serve a God who wants us to be
whole, not oppressed. What does that mean for people of
color? Let me share five segments in the cycle toward wholeness that I have found helpful when I talk about systemic
transformation.

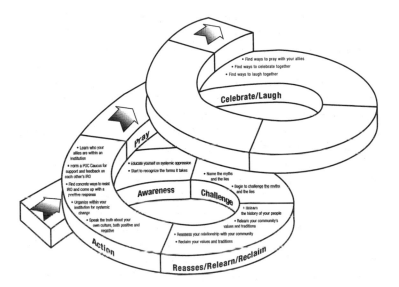

As in any journey toward wholeness, we must first become aware of our oppression, and not just aware, but, we must also recognize how we participate in it, what we feel, and how we name the experience. We need to be able to recognize the myths and lies if we are going to work toward wholeness. The naming of our oppression is essential in beginning the journey.

In the second segment, we need to have courage to start challenging the myths and lies. We can no longer afford to sit quietly, unless we are ready to give up. I do not mean that we are responsible for educating the dominant culture. Rather, we are responsible for educating our people and ourselves. During my youngest daughter's sophomore year of high school, her social studies teacher showed a very racist movie about Muslim people. My daughter was offended by the movie and came home upset. I could have told her that her teacher was wrong and left it at that. But if I did, what would I be teaching my daughter? My husband and I chose to confront the teacher and gave him an article that reviewed the movie as reinforcing racism. We didn't confront for the edification of the white teacher, we did it to teach my daughter that misinformation about a people must be challenged.

Along with challenging the myths and lies, as people of color, we need to relearn, reassess, reclaim, and celebrate our values and traditions. Some may say that to do that is a lot of work. But isn't it a lot of work to continually live with the myths and lies? During the last two years I have been digging through historical documents about Aztecs, and I have been able to make some links between my worldview in relationship to my Aztec ancestry. I know where I fit in the world. I am learning what unique gifts I can bring to the body of Christ. I can celebrate who I am. This segment is the food, the nourishment we will need to continue working toward systemic transformation. This piece of rediscovery is essential in our transformation as Christians. We must be able to know who we are and who our Creator intended us to be in this world.

In an institutional setting, the fourth segment, systemic transformation, requires organizing people of color to speak the truth about who they are, what they need, and how they are affected by oppression. If there is to be true mutuality in the future, we will need to openly challenge white people to educate themselves about our cultures and histories, just as we have had to educate ourselves about theirs. In the challenging, we must also present our alternative worldview, a worldview that does not revolve around power and wealth.

As people of color, we will also need to speak truthfully about the positive and negative aspects of our culture. For example, as Christians our communities need to discern the ways in which we can worship and glorify God that are culturally appropriate within our communities. If our culture oppresses others within or outside our culture, we must also address those issues. No culture is perfect, but each has a place in God's kingdom.

The final segment is a time of praying, celebrating, and laughing with our co-strugglers and other people of color as we work together in addressing racism and internalized racist oppression within our institutions. I believe these elements of joy should run through the entire journey toward wholeness.

Using the spiral paradigm introduced in chapter 4, I want to explore four specific areas that are quite destructive to us as people of color in institutional settings. Donna K. Bivens from the Women's Theological Center in Boston wrote that internalized racist oppression "involves at least four essential and interconnected elements": decision making, resources, standards, and naming the problem.[1] As we begin to look at these elements keep in mind that, as entrenched and interconnected as these elements are, God is able to set us free.

Decision making

As people of color we must first recognize what the myth is regarding decision making. We have been conditioned to believe that white people know what is best for us and our communities. As people of color, we are rewarded when we support the myth and punished if we resist or challenge the myth.

Institutions make decisions

Two of the major systems making decisions for people of color have been the educational system and the church. One example is the common practice in our high schools in the United States of tracking students. When students of color do not learn well and are not able to cope well in a white educational model, one of two things happens. Either they are put in special education or steered toward vocational training. Many times parents go along with the decisions, not because they do not care about their children, but because they have been conditioned to believe that the white educational structure knows what is best for their children. The power to make such decisions about our children will affect them all their lives.

A friend of mine, who is Latina, shared with me her experience in a graduate course on special education. In a section on multicultural education centered around the issue of restoration, it was taught that if a student in special education had lost her native language and culture, it was the teacher's responsibility to restore the language and culture back to the student. In most instances, the teacher would most likely be white, not from the student's own culture. Can a basically white-controlled institution restore the student's culture? Shouldn't that be the parents' decision? Shouldn't the child's community be involved in the restoration?

This example is the flip side of my own story. I was put into speech class so I would not have an accent that would hinder me in my educational process. I remember being confused in first grade about why such a big deal was made about the "sh" sound instead of the "ch" sound. Was it worth the stress and grief? Why weren't other accents targeted besides Spanish? I remember spending extra time on learning to read and trying to catch up with my white friends. By the time I reached fourth grade I had caught up, but by that time my self-esteem was shot. Humiliating a young child because of her accent is very devastating. No one ever explained why it took me longer to become a good reader. The school never praised me for having two languages but constantly criticized my lack of perfection in the English language. When I finally mastered English, the school system turned around and wondered why I wasn't doing better in my Spanish class.

The type of day-to-day decisions schools make for children of color are destroying them. My daughter, a junior in high school, comes home with the same type of stories I had to live through as a child. My daughter has an advantage of being far more aware of the institutional racism within our schools, so she is able to resist some of the consequences. But the reality is our children will have a hard time escaping completely unscathed.

In a magazine article in *ColorLines*, Jesse Jackson was interviewed about the two-year expulsion of seven African-American boys involved in a 17-second fight where no weapons were involved. The school board decided, without due process, to expel the students for two years. Two of the students were seniors with less than four credits to graduate. I am not advocating for no discipline, but the standard punishment for a fight of that nature would have been 10 days. In a time where children of color are dropping out of school, why would a school make such a decision?

The action was taken by a school board of six whites and one black. The town's third largest employer is the school district. Though the population of the city is 16 percent black, the school student body is 40 percent children of color. Many white people who send their children to private academies still vote for the public school board. Jackson said, "Every position of influence is held by a white person—the counselors, the contractors, the vendors, and the school board officers, and 95 percent of the teachers—every position of power."[2]

These decisions, made by institutions, are powerful and destructive to people of color. I know my parents did what the school told them because they wanted us to get a good education. I want to be clear: the system is set up for people of color to allow white institutions to make major decisions for us. We go along for several reasons: (1) fear of the consequences of not going along, (2) believing that the white institution really does know what's better for us, and (3) for the little and short-lived rewards we might get for cooperating with the system.

The consequences for naming the racism within institutions are real. In the example of the expelled students, the school board was challenged for their first decision and later they reduced the expulsion to one year, again without due process. But they retaliated. The school board released the tape of the fight to CBS, got the state attorney to file charges, and released the students' private records which is against the law. No wonder we, as people of color, hesitate to challenge the educational system. It is a very powerful system.

Resistance to institutional decision making

Sometimes, norms within an institution may not apply to

people of color. I remember when people of color decided to address the issue of racism within a particular institution. After several failed attempts at trying to voice our concerns individually we decided to write a joint memo. Memos carry a lot of weight in white institutions, and the people of color were well aware that joint memo writing was a norm used by the white people in the institution and felt it was a valid form to use to address our concerns. As you can imagine there was quite a reaction to the memo. One of the responses I found quite troubling was when a supervisor went to one of the contributors and asked why we hadn't each done an individual memo, saying that that would have been the best way for us to have handled the situation. When the supervisor was asked why white people were allowed to write joint letters but people of color were now being told they should have written individual memos, the conversation ended. The institution would have liked to find a way to lessen the power of a collective memo written by people of color, but we did not back away even though there was tremendous pressure to do so.

There is tremendous pressure to go along with a decision that has already been made. I do not want to in any way judge my sisters and brothers of color when they do not resist unjust and ethnocentric decisions made for them. These pressures take a toll on our mental and physical health, as well as our general well-being. But I do want to find ways for us to use our resistance and organization as part of our journey toward wholeness.

From its first interactions with people of color, the church has made decisions for people of color, not the least of these being the introduction of Christianity clothed in Western thought and culture. Decisions concerning our ancestors' conversion and way of life were made for them. The church made decisions to burn most of the indigenous writings in Mexico and part of what is now the United States. First Nations people were sent to boarding schools, many of which were owned by the church. If indigenous culture did not fit into the defined Western Christian expression, the church made decisions to enforce compliance. I am sure if we look into decisions surrounding funding patterns for churches of people of color and programs in the church, we will find similar correlations around compliance to Western church standards even today.

In his book *Columbus and Other Cannibals*, Jack Forbes contended that the only people of color group in the United States that has been able to develop an authentic form of Christianity are African-Americans. He says, "Brought over from Europe, they have succeeded in developing a 'spirit living,' based upon suffering, sharing, and humility, which permeates their faith." He goes on to say, "If you heard the late Martin Luther King Jr. speak, you must know that you are experiencing the true potential of Christianity in the United States."[3]

Out of the African-American experience collective resistance was able to form a deep spiritual understanding of Christianity. Unfortunately, other groups have adopted Western Christianity leaving their spiritual-cultural understandings behind. I hope we are at a point in history where we can recover a collective understanding of who we are, in my case, as a Mexic-Amerindian. We need to collectively make decisions for ourselves within institutional settings whether in the classroom, workplace, church, or at the bank. We must collectively question decisions that are made, supposedly, on our behalf which destroy who we are. An essential part of this will be organizing ourselves. Chapter 6 will further develop ways to organize for systemic transformation.

The biblical passage in Matthew 4:1-11 tells the story of Jesus' own resistance to what the "world" had to offer him. Jesus resisted because he knew who he was and he was clear why he was sent to the earth. He was also clear as to who he was to serve, "the Lord your God." In order for Jesus to serve, he first had to resist the world, which was presented to him as symbols of wealth and power.

The word "resistance" is not a dirty word. It is a word that has meant survival for indigenous cultures and other oppressed people throughout the world. Internalized racist oppression must be resisted on three levels by people of color: the personal, the community, and institutional/systemic levels. As Jesus resisted evil, we too must resist the misinformation, missing information, and biased history and stereotypes about who we are. We must name and display the gifts we bring to our society, including the church. If we fail to do that for ourselves we will deny the kingdom of God of its fullness and we will destroy ourselves as a people.

People of color have been tempted to give up who they are for the promise of the "American Dream." A few of us succeed in obtaining that dream to some extent, but we often find it lacking, shallow, and empty. We often end up paying a very heavy price; we pay with the destruction of who we were created to be in this world.

6

Continuing the Journey: dispelling the myth

Then the woman, knowing what had happened to her, came and fell at his feet and, trembling with fear, told him the whole truth. He said to her, "Daughter, your faith has healed you. Go in peace and be freed from your suffering."
(Mark 5:33-34 NIV)

In chapter 5 we began the journey toward wholeness by looking at decision making, the first of the four elements of internalized racist oppression. As we continue on this journey, we will explore the last three elements: resources, standards, and naming the problem, and the overall task of dispelling the myth of internalized racist oppression.

Resources

When talking about resources and standards I will mainly focus on the issues around access, control, and the lessons we, as people of color, have been taught by the dominant culture in the United States. Concerning resources, we have been fed the myth that by using resources for ourselves and in our communities we are not serving everybody. With the stigma against "freeloaders" in this society it is very hard for us to use resources on ourselves and our communities without feeling selfish and guilty.

Dispelling the myth and confronting the truth

The myth we must first confront is the myth that we are not entitled to the resources because we are lazy, inferior, and freeloaders. The truth of the matter is that the dominant culture used the labor of people of color, either by slavery or exploitative labor practices, used stolen land, and orchestrated the genocide of the indigenous population of the United States to create the United States. Some of these same methods are being used today, sometimes in subtle ways and sometimes blatant.

The farmworkers in the United States continue to be some of the lowest paid workers, and yet their work is one of the most labor-intensive jobs. It is ridiculous to view farmworkers as lazy or as people wanting to rip off the system. The reality of why we don't have a closed southern border has to do in part with the demand for farmworkers in the United States. United States growers know that they will not find enough workers in the dominant culture to fulfill their labor needs.

When we, as people of color, start to relearn our history it will begin to liberate us from believing we are not entitled to access and control of resources. When I say access and control, I don't necessarily mean access and control in the same way that dominant culture uses the terms. I do not believe that the work we do in our journey toward wellness is to have exactly what the dominant culture has, but rather to be able to have access and control for our self-determination. My hope is that our worldviews will be seen as another piece of humanity in the created order, that we may find ways to "cut the pie" other than in a hierarchical order.

If we buy into the idea that the pie can only be cut in a hierarchical manner, we too start to practice exploitative ways of using people; we see it happen within our own neighborhoods. We must work hard for the betterment of all people and not just ourselves. Mexican-Americans born in the United States cannot see themselves as better than our Mexican brothers and sister new to this country. When we fight against each other to preserve our limited benefits and privileges, we have allowed the system of internalized racism to win and neither group becomes free.

Access and control

A couple of years ago a mother came to my office. She knew that I was actively involved in antiracism work and wanted to share her story with me. She is a first-generation immigrant and has an education, but because of her accent people assume she is uneducated. Her son started kindergarten and was struggling in school. Her experience of her son was one of a happy, energetic boy but she was getting another story from the school and the boy she heard described was not the son she knew. She asked the teacher if she thought something was wrong with him and the teacher replied, "No, he's just a misbehaved little boy."

The mother told me that her son struggled through kindergarten and started first grade. Problems at the school began to escalate. The combination of constantly being put down and scolded by the teachers began to take a toll on her son's personality. She asked about testing and was told that only teachers could request testing and that the school saw no need for the tests. In desperation, she took her son to a therapist who informed her that she could request testing from the school and that they had to comply with her request within 30 days. Here was a mother, with limited resources, who had to pay an outside doctor to get information the school should have shared with her. After her son was tested, he was diagnosed with borderline autism that explained a lot of his behavior. Now, not only does he have to learn to live with his autism, but he also has to overcome the self-esteem damage done by the educational system.

This story directly applies to issues of access. The behavior of the school, which is not an isolated incident, made the mother feel like she had to beg for help, that for some unknown reason her son was not entitled to the resources available. People of color should not feel ashamed of using resources. Yet each time we try to access resources, institutions set up roadblocks.

In a skit done by Eddie Murphy, he was disguised as a white man. His purpose was to discover just how many resources are available to white people. The skit is a parody of the book *Black Like Me* in which a white man becomes black to discover the racism experienced by black men. For people of color, the skit is painfully hilarious because even though it's funny we know there is truth in the skit. In one scene, Eddie Murphy went into the bank to get a loan. The loan officer, an African-American male, started to refuse the loan due to Eddie's lack of employment. Suddenly, the loan officer was relieved by his supervisor, a white male. The white supervisor laughed, sat down, and said to Eddie, "Boy that was a close call." He then proceeded to ask Eddie how much he needed and handed over piles of money. We all know the skit is extreme, but there is truth nonetheless.

Couple the lack of resources for your community with lack of decision-making power and what do you get? An oppressed community that is powerless. The same scenario of low amounts of resources being made available to people of color groups is played out in our church settings. Also, the type of controls put on those resources are based on mostly white decision-making bodies. I am constantly amazed at how white people are plugged into the different sources and have access to money for education, work, church, and pleasure.

We must recognize that use of the resources should be made available to people of color, especially in the church. With the resources must come the freedom to make decisions, for our worldview to be respected, and the ability for us to speak the truth of our oppression. Historically we have spent our energy in fighting for the crumbs instead of uniting with other people of color and challenging the distribution of all the resources.

We, as people of color, must realize and confess our own misuse of resources by allowing the internalization of what we have been taught to become reality. We have allowed lies like "you are people who do not know how to handle money" to play out in the choices we have made in our communities and churches. We must resist those lies and take responsibility for ourselves.

After claiming responsibility, we must make sure we make responsible and wise choices. We need to work together to discover what is really important to our communities. We need to focus on basic needs that make us healthy human beings, which include our spiritual, mental, and physical well-being. All the other things, such as material wealth, are excesses. Many of our cultures come with communal or familial understandings and are not based on individualism. These are the values that could be a gift to our church, communities, and society at large. When we look at resources with a communal and familial worldview, it can give us a different way of looking at resources. Resources can be viewed as a tool to help achieve our communal and familial responsibilities instead of viewing resources as the means to an individual end.

Standards
Dispelling the myth

Who sets the standards and norms in our society? What is seen as appropriate and normal? Questioning the standards is also about people of color not being able to live up to their deepest values and the difficulty we have in naming, communicating, and holding ourselves and each other accountable to them. The myth we face is that the values and standards set by the white dominant culture in the United States is superior, normal, appropriate, (and/or) correct, and all other standards and values are inferior.

It is very hard to live up to standards and norms that go directly against what you believe. But people of color are asked to do that on a daily basis, "24/7" as my youngest daughter would say. As people of color, we have helped enforce the standards and values of the dominant culture because we have come to believe the standards and norms are superior and normal. This is the same kind of thinking that allows a southern border to separate us from our homeland, and First Nations people to be separated at both borders. It allows some of us to join the anti-immigration sentiment of the United States against our own Mexican brothers and sisters and accept the standards that allows school systems to make decisions for our children that have lifelong consequences. This myth is also connected to how we use resources. Whose way of spending is right? Whose standards do we use to decide on issues around decision making and resources? This web of internalized racist oppression is all interconnected.

Learning who we are and what we believe will give us greater understanding to what is important to us as a people. As a Mexic-Amerindian, I believe we have something to contribute that would help bring our world into balance, but we are unaware of the gifts our Mexican culture could bring. The following paragraph, found in the book *500 Years of Chicano History*, gives a brief account of what we could bring.

> Our birth as a people goes back to the time when Mexico was home to societies noted for splendid art and architecture, a belief in environmental harmony, and scientific wonders. It was a land of ancient cultures that prohibited anyone going hungry and homeless. The idea of land as private property did not exist; how could you buy mother of life? People respected cooperation—not competition. Such were the communal, spiritual values of indigenous people up and down this continent.[1]

One of the things I've come to realize is that each culture's standards are a gift. For example, let's look at the various views of relationships and work. We all know that in the United States there is much said about white people's work ethic, and that everyone else's work ethic is measured according to this model standard. The fact is that the ancestral homeland of white people is Europe and due to the climate of Europe, some groups had a very limited planting time and harvest time. Their survival depended on how much they could do within a limited time period so they became conditioned to produce as much as possible within a short span of time.

My ancestry is from Mexico where the climate is much more temperate year round and at times can be very hot. Our work ethic is one of moderation with an emphasis on relationships. Our survival was not dependent on time since we had plenty to eat year round. Our time was spent cultivating relationships and strengthening familial and communal ties.[2]

These are two very different ways of seeing work. It is not a matter of asking which is better, but of seeing equal value in both standards. Can we see times where a Mexican work ethic would be a gift to those consumed with producing at the expense of their families? Can we see there will be times when working with time limits is essential? When we are asked to live by only one standard all the time, we discount the gift of another culture that is just as valid and is desperately needed to give balance. When it is one group's norms and standards that are held up in our churches, educational system, government, economic system, health care systems, and others, we lose the opportunity to learn different ways of doing things that could provide a much richer experience. As people of color, we must also be mindful of how those standards and norms may be used against us in the workplace, at school, at the bank, and in many other institutions. We must realize that dominant culture standards were not put in place for our benefit. We must stop believing that in order to be part of this society, we must submit to the standards and norms that actually bring harm to who we are as a people group.

Our compliance, whether through active deeds or just keeping quiet, helps this massive machinery of racism to continue consuming us. We can point the finger at the churches' silence or the silence of our society, but we must also deal with our own silence. As Christians we must be willing to follow the radical Jesus who stood against the political and social powers of his time. Can we, as people of color, take responsibility in helping the church continue to develop counter ways of being the body of Christ instead of allowing the dominant society to dictate the shape of the church? The body of Christ must include all nations, tribes, tongues, and languages; we must all be represented to truly reflect the church.

In my experience within Mennonite churches, I have often seen churches of color try to model the white church in worship. I have often heard churches of color referred to as "not being" Mennonite because of their form of worship or how they operate as a church. Oftentimes, decisions are made on resources according to how they "fit" the standard of what is viewed as Mennonite. Resources are also allocated with the "assumption" that the group receiving the resources will operate in a manner consistent with the dominant culture's viewpoint.

I am not advocating doing away with accountability structures, but I would hope that we could find many ways of being accountable that would be inclusive of other world-views about time, relationships, work, and money. People of color must start to think outside of what has been presented to us as the "norm" and start presenting, with confidence, alternative ways of doing things. People of color need to provide viable alternatives, or at least a place to start a conversation.

As people of color, we are beyond complaining about what we don't have. We need to identify what we need to be healthy human beings. I believe we can find some creative alternatives for ourselves and our society.

What's in a name?

Naming is such a powerful act. As I shared earlier, even the ability to name yourself has transformative spiritual significance. What would naming on an institutional level mean? What type of transformation would be possible?

Before we can look at the transformative piece of naming, we must look at what has happened in the last 500 years in the United States with naming. Most institutions in the United States, with very few exceptions, were created to serve white people. Schools were set up to educate the children of white settlers. Puritans and others left the United Kingdom for religious freedom over doctrine, and churches were quickly set up in the early colonies. As more and more white settlers moved to the Americas, more and more institutions were set up to meet their needs.

The Christian church, both Protestant and Catholic, was eager to convert the "savages." The naming had already begun. Peoples from the Americas that had progressive ancient societies were being named savages because their ways were not the way of the white settlers. Richard Twiss, a Lakota writer and Christian, says "After 500 years of active missionary effort, most missiologists agree that only three to five percent of the Native population are born-again Christians.... In short an authentic Native American cultural expression of Christianity has never been allowed to develop—the very idea has been rejected. Is it any wonder many native people now view Christianity as the 'white man's religion,' and blame Christians for the loss of their own culture and identity?"[3]

As people of color, we have allowed the dominant culture to name our Christian expression of faith, our theology, and our Christian practices for us. Dancing, for example, is taboo in many Christian denominations, so our traditional dances have become evil instead of being redeemed within our cultures as a way to worship and glorify God. We have converted hymns to our language and called them our faith expression. Where is the music of our own traditions when we worship God?

We must believe that our ways of doing things, whether in worship or how we work, has value. It not only has value, but is a gift to society. The freedom to worship God within our own cultural understanding could allow others to value their own culture and who they are as a people. I will not deny the power that the dominant culture has in naming our societies.

Things that had significant value in our society were often taught as being evil or inferior. We have come to believe that the white dominant culture knows what is best for us. We are silenced or ignored in our attempts to name within institutions, whether the church or the educational system, and we are left to feel powerless. We must resist their naming because it is only God as our Creator who can name who we are.

In 1998, PBS had an eight-hour special on the Mexican-American War. I wasn't quite sure whether I wanted to watch it because in south Texas and the Southwest it is clear that the United States stole our land. Yes, the educational system tells us differently, but we know another reality. I decided to watch it and was surprised that it included two Mexican historians commenting on the documentary. The one thing that stuck in my head for days was something Walt Whitman said about the Mexicans. In essence, he wondered how Mexicans could actually believe that white people could govern side-by-side with an inferior race like Mexicans. I asked myself why that particular part of the documentary stuck with me, and realized that it was because here was a writer I was taught to revere as a "great American writer," who had no respect for my people. His freedom and power to name and be quoted carried significant weight. Of course I got angry and felt powerless in hearing those words, but I am here to tell you that we no longer need to feel defeated and powerless. We need to find ways to organize ourselves in order to name our own realities as valid ways to see and do things in our workplace, in the church, and in society at large.

In the reading of Mark 4:1-20, I am always struck with Jesus' resistance to power and wealth. The "American dream" is the ever-present carrot dangled in front of people of color. I do not want the American dream in exchange for who God has created me to be in this world. The lie behind the American dream for people of color is that some of us may obtain a part of that dream, but we will never be seen as equals in our society. So I must find ways to resist the temptation.

One is the loneliest number

There are times where you will find yourself the only voice in the naming of racism. Sometimes a brother or sister of color publicly reinforces a value of the dominant culture that makes people of color look inferior. Do your brother or sister a favor and tell them. Share with them how they reinforced the racism within the institution and how that also further worked to colonize people of color.

A good example of this was when I sat on a board that was looking for ways to increase the number of people of color on the board. A white person suggested that we could use a "Paul and Timothy" model in order to teach people of color how to be on boards. As all the white people agreed it was a great idea, a brother of color also agreed. I spoke up and asked what made people think that people of color did not know how to be on boards? Citing my years of board experience, I assured the people that many people of color are active on many boards in their communities. Later I took my brother aside and asked him if he thought that his affirming that people of color needed to be trained to sit on boards helped to further the stereotypes. I also admitted that if I had not been aware of what was going on, I could have further internalized the stereotype of people of color myself.

How we name collectively

When we decide to name the racism within an institution and among ourselves, it will be important to remember that there is strength in numbers. When a major way of doing things or a decision is made that furthers racism in an institution, we need to find ways to work collectively with other people of color in the institution.

1. Caucus with other people of color and white co-strugglers. Name the situation to the group and ask for their perspective. If there seems to be a general consensus, the next question is whether the racism should be named to the institution. Naming to the institution is not just the naming of the problem, but also naming with correct information and concrete antiracist solutions.

2. Make sure that everyone is in agreement with naming the reality. We must ask ourselves if we are willing to lose our jobs over it. Someone in the group may not be in a position to lose his or her job. Are there ways we can protect that person's job? Maybe some people in the group will have to silently support through prayer. Remember there is no shame in having to protect your job. Many people of color do not come with generational wealth and we are talking about survival. We cannot divide ourselves into who can take a chance and who can't. The next time it could be me or you who must silently pray for the others.

3. Be clear on what the issue is and give specific examples. We cannot be swayed when others point to the exceptions. One example when talking about power: One way to measure power in our society, including the church, is to look where the majority of the money is. Who has the say as to how it is used? Unfortunately, in the United States, money is power.

4. Be prepared with proactive alternatives that will be inclusive of people of color. Do not settle for tokenism or exceptions. Remember, in naming for ourselves, we are giving a gift.

5. Don't expect big changes. Our naming will have to become a generational process, just as the naming by the colonizers has been going on for the last 500 years in the Americas. Even though I say don't expect big changes, expect God to transform you in the process. Know that God wants us to be whole.

6. When you feel that you were unable to speak up and you allowed someone to misname your experience, don't be ashamed, because the fact is that sometimes we don't even realize our reality has been misnamed. We often participate in promoting unhealthy ways for ourselves and bringing privilege and benefit to the dominant culture without being aware of it.

We need to be willing to share our struggle as gatekeepers and co-conspirators in our resistance to internalized racist oppression. We have had enough shame dumped on us as people of color that it is now time to speak openly with each other, not to blame or shame, but to encourage and lift each other up. We must be able to name corporately our reality to institutions that have the power to name in ways that damage our souls. We must be willing to speak up instead of silently allowing the dominant culture to misname for us.

The ability to start naming for ourselves begins by recognizing what is being named and what is being ignored. Remember that awareness is the first step. Begin to start recognizing patterns that name the dominant culture's reality but are harmful to you. Once you begin to recognize the misnaming of your experience, learn to hear the stereotypes, misinformation, missing information, and biased history being used to name and keep people of color oppressed.

Relearn your community's values and traditions in light of your history. Reclaim who you are so that you can accurately name who you are in a collective effort with other oppressed people of color. Know that by naming, you are resisting internalized racist oppression and becoming the person God created you to be.

7

Who Are White People?

When Jesus saw that he answered wisely, he said to him, "You are not far from the kingdom of God." After that no one dared to ask him any question.
(Mark 12:34 NRSV)

The sun sauntered across his forehead. Had he been there forever, instead of only an afternoon, he would look no different. Time ran thick across skin the color of rich soil. His face, a clock stuck between one minute and the next.

Into the long night he sat, until, achingly curious, neighbors on either side heard him:

I don't know what I am. I thought I knew, but I don't know.

I wasn't seeking revelation. I just overheard the Sadducees' question: "Seven brothers. One wife. Who will be married in heaven?" I saw he answered well, "He is God not of the dead, but of the living; you are quite wrong."

So I asked my own question. Not to trap him. I wanted to know what he thought.

"Which commandment is the first of all?"

I thought he would say the Shema and stop. He didn't.
He didn't stop with, "The Lord our God, the Lord is one;
you shall love the Lord your God with all your heart,
and with all your soul, and with all your mind, and with
all your strength." He went on:
The second is this, "You shall love your neighbor as
yourself." There is no other commandment greater than
these.
And I saw he was right. Even though I didn't want to.
Even though I knew he was trying to tell me, a scribe,
that I and those like me have not loved our neighbors
well. I knew that. Yes, we are the ones who get respect in
the marketplace, in synagogues, at banquets. Some of us
say long prayers to look good. And some of us gain from
the poor, the oppressed, even widows. I knew it then. I
know it now.
Then I told him that loving God and neighbor as self
were greater than all whole burnt offerings and sacrifices.
I did not argue with him. I agreed. I said he was right.
So I do not understand.

Neighbors at their thresholds paused with him, for fear
that he wait another night before next speaking. His hands
and voice trembled as he went on.

This Jesus, this rural rabbi, who did answer well told me
that I was not "far from the kingdom."
I don't know who I am.
All my life I have followed the rules, lived within the
boundaries of right conduct, listened to truth even when
it comes from the most unlikely of sources.
But "not far from the kingdom"? Not yet in? Almost,
but not quite. Who am I that I have not yet entered?
What else does he think I need to do? Am I so unwell?
Knowing the heart of this good man, his neighbors
shake their heads in indignation. This Jesus is a trouble-
maker.[1]

Where the journey starts

Every journey starts from a place we know. This book is a journey into racism's effect on white people and people of color. I begin my part of the journey with an unnamed scribe whom Jesus said was "not far from the kingdom" because I know him well. He is, like me, a white person.

This scribe's identity parallels white people's identity today. White people also "are the ones who get respect in the marketplace and in the synagogues and at the banquets." Some of us do "say long prayers." All of us, by virtue of our skin color, "end up gaining from the poor, the oppressed, even widows." Those white privileges shape our identity.

And, like the scribe, we face a similar dilemma. Sometimes after acknowledging the power and privilege we receive, we ask, "Is that not enough?" As one white high school senior blurted out in the midst of a Bible study, "What else do you want?" Paraphrasing this nameless scribe, "Are we really not far from the kingdom? Is something keeping us from entering in? Are we so unwell?"

I believe that scribes are white people because Jesus describes them as being beneficiaries, the privileged ones, in a society that oppressed the poor, defined some as clean and others not so, and made certain that those on the top stayed there. And since I know this to be true of white people as well, I pay very close attention to what Jesus says to scribes.

After an otherwise positive exchange, in fact the only place in Mark where Jesus' interaction with a scribe is not entirely negative, Jesus still does not invite him in. He is only near. Surely he is not far, but he is also not yet in. Jesus seems to be suggesting that to enter the kingdom of God, something more must happen. Perhaps he, like the rest of the scribes, needs healing. Perhaps they are too sick to know they are not yet in the kingdom.

In an age where political correctness runs rampant, youthful cynicism defines a generation, and racism sends a message that all is well, Jesus speaks to us who are white. He knows what holds us back. He invites us to enter in.

Healthy white people

My son Zachary and I found ourselves in a West Philadelphia park one rainy afternoon. As Zachary tossed a Frisbee, I pushed my friend Jeff's daughter Katie in a stroller. While Zachary chased a wild toss, Jeff asked me, "So what are white people supposed to do? What do you want to become?"

Because I trust Jeff as a fellow white male struggling to live out antiracist commitments, I gave his question careful consideration.

As Zachary pushed Katie's stroller, I said, "I want to be a healthy white person." This was the first time I had articulated that thought. Yet even as I said it, I knew that I had only begun to discover what it meant. And so to discover more, I took my questions to a very practical place, the world of a second-grader.

The morning is Wednesday, November 17, 1999. Zachary John Shearer is squirming on my lap. I have informed this seven-year-old that he is going to help me write a book chapter. All he has to do is answer five simple questions without wiggling too much. Here is the transcript of our interview:

Dad: Zachary, what does it mean when someone is healthy?

Zachary: You eat vegetables and fruits. You exercise. That's all I can think of.

Dad: Okay, now what does it mean if someone is a white person?

Zachary: Um, that their skin color is the color white. [Shoulder shrug.] I don't know what else.

Dad: Are white people more healthy than people of color?

Zachary: No.

Dad: Why not?

Zachary: Because no matter what color your skin is you can be as healthy as a person with a different color of skin.

Dad: I see I can only ask one more question. I guess I better make it a good one. Zachary, what's the best way you know of to stop racism?

Zachary: Oh no. This is a hard one. [Long pause.] To make a friend of anybody who has a different color of skin.
Dad: Come on. You can think of one more thing.
Zachary: No, you just said five questions and I'm not going to think of two answers to one of them.

This is the child who, when three years old, informed me, "I'm glad you're helping to stop people erase each other." Although that tenderness is now often replaced by burgeoning independence, he still understands a basic truth about racism. No one should be any healthier than anyone else. That is the way it should be.

However, it is not.

The work is harder and more demanding than Zachary knows. It requires much more than exercise and a proper diet of fruits and vegetables. To be a healthy white person who has found a measure of healing in a racist society, who acts out of that healing, and who carries out antiracist action in the private and the political, to be such a person requires much more. As Zachary and I talked, it finally came to me what that is. It requires knowing who we are.

Know who we are

To be healthy as white people, we need to know who we are. Part of that knowledge comes from discovering how our whiteness hurts us, how it keeps us from entering the kingdom. And to gain that knowledge, we need to understand both the individual and corporate dimensions of what blocks our entrance. The next three chapters explore what blocks us and how we can move forward: Who are white people? (chapter 7), How does whiteness hurt us? (chapter 8), and finally, How do we respond? (chapter 9).

Throughout these chapters, I will refer to four spaces[2] we white people need to explore. Each of these spaces or themes carries principal tasks. I will introduce both spaces and tasks here, describe the spaces in chapter 8, and expand on the tasks in chapter 9.

Four white spaces

Isolation. We white people have a difficult time understanding that we are part of a group. Our first, almost instinctual response is to isolate ourselves as individuals. While this may be true for Western society in the main, my observation is that this impulse is amplified and warped in white people.

In the space of isolation, the task is connecting. Here I am identifying a group task, even more than individual tasks. We must together understand that we are a group of people who have all been shaped into being white.

Control. For many of us, this space is the most difficult to visit. We do not want to acknowledge how used we are to being in control. We want to be able to define the problem, solution, and response to racism. We do not want to open ourselves to the spiritual dimensions or effects of racism on our lives. We want everything to be under our tangible, logical control.

In the space of control, the task is letting go. The collective task here is to let go of control by grounding ourselves in God, not racism. We are called to not only give up personal control through individual actions, but to restructure our congregations and institutions so that we are not constantly placed in positions of control.

Loss. In the process of becoming white, European-Americans lost much of our culture and history. We disowned an intimate understanding of where we come from and how we came to be. We lost a story to tell. Just as the people of Israel had to be reminded again and again of where they came from and how they came to be the children of Israel, to do so we as white people need a similar story of foundation.

In the space of loss, the task is finding. To be healthy white people, we need to find our history. When, where, and how was language lost? What cultural specificity disappeared and when? Who were the resisters who did not want to succumb to whiteness? What were their names? Where was God in the midst of these stories?

Loathing. One of the more curious spaces that racism creates for white people is self-loathing and an active distaste for and mistrust of other white people. I have wondered already if some of the more ardent white antiracists are ever able to sit down and simply enjoy being with a group of other white people. It does us no good if in the midst of working to dismantle racism we end up loathing each other.

In the space of loathing, the task is loving. This task is most easily open to misinterpretation. I am not talking about a simple feel-good-be-nice-never-offend-challenge-or-proclaim sort of love. Instead, I refer here to a love that cares deeply about other white people. I am talking about a vulnerable speak-truth-stick-with-be-there-hang-on-laugh-weep-struggle sort of love. I am also talking about the task that is most challenging for me on an individual basis. I would not be surprised to discover that it is the most difficult group task as well.

Entering the kingdom

Underlying each of these spaces is the pattern of superiority racism teaches us. If we know nothing else about being white, we need to know that we have been taught to believe we have the answers. Like the unnamed scribe at the doorstep, it can shake us to our very foundations to discover that these lessons of superiority, and the ensuing dependence on privilege, may inhibit our complete and unlimited entrance to the kingdom.

The pressures to conform to whiteness are enormous. Often severe penalties are put in place if we do stretch the boundaries.[3] The question before us is whether we can wrestle with whiteness until we have found a way to be white that does not require superiority, does not necessitate dependence on privilege, does not leave us so ill that we don't know we're outside the kingdom.

Here are four questions, one for each white space, to help us discover who white people are:

Isolation: How do I know who I am? Think over the last

week. Identify who has told you who you are. My sons have told me that I am father (and an unfair one at that). Cheryl told me that I was the only one she loved. Colleagues at work reminded me, half in jest, half seriously, that I am white and "wouldn't understand." Members of my congregation's youth group informed me that I am old.

Many messages, and most of them positive. There have been other more subtle messages, however. The magazines at the grocery store told me that white women are the most beautiful. The newspaper said the real decision makers look like me. An early morning pass by a police cruiser left me feeling protected. People who look like me overpopulated too many television channels.

Here I am told that I am one of "us." I am told I belong. I am told I am we and we are the best. I am told I am white. As Judith Levine notes, "Whiteness is everything and nothing. It is the race that need not speak its name."[4]

But I have also known this week that I am loved by God. I have known that regardless of what racism seeks daily to reinforce, I am wonderfully loved by God. It matters immensely what I do in response to how I am known, but none of it changes how much God loves me. I am a child of God. I need not be isolated anymore.

Control: How do I know sin? Think about what you know of sin. Identify where you see it. Examine not only the personal sins of omission and commission in family, work, and church life, but also those systemic sins that harm the planet, destroy the possibility of personal redemption, and that keep poverty, ill-health, and violence alive and well. Consider how racism is one sin at the root of many of those deaths, both small and large.

Likewise, racism's expression in white privilege and internalized racist superiority is inherently sinful. I make that suggestion not to compartmentalize these forces in the realm of the interpersonal. Neither do I want to haul my white sisters and brothers into a morass of guilt. But I am concerned here that we say clearly, with the best of the theological language we have to offer, that racism in all its forms is contrary to the purposes of God. The provision of privileges for white people is sin. Any individual, institutional, or systemic expression of white superiority is also sin. Such knowledge, to paraphrase the psalmist, is better than any burnt offering. It gives us a basis for letting go in the white space of control and grounding ourselves in God's presence.

Loss: How near do you sit to the kingdom? I opened this chapter with an imagined story of a scribe sitting at home after having been told by Jesus that he was not far from the kingdom. By asking the question here, I want to focus in as concrete a manner as I know how that our response to our whiteness is directly connected with our ability to fully enter the kingdom. Take this not as a time to debate with yourself or others (or me) about the nature of salvation. Use it instead to ponder the ways in which racism throws down constant barriers to entering the kingdom Jesus here names.

Notice any emotions that this question may arouse. Spend time searching for the roots of those feelings. Emotions I have felt when others have posed this question to me in this or similar forms include defensiveness, anger, sadness, and relief (at the truth being spoken so clearly). Honor the emotions, but do not let them detract you from the purpose at hand. Remember you are searching inside about the effects of racism on you as a white person, in order to prepare yourself for effective response to this demon.

Think also of Paul's writings about the principalities and powers. Consider which ways the gift of human diversity have been warped and transformed to not only jeopardize white people's entrance into the kingdom, but also oppress, demean, and diminish people of color on a regular basis. Examine where you sit in relationship to the kingdom. Identify what role racism has played in putting you there. What have you lost as you became white?

Loathing: How do I respond to sin? For much of my life I have been uncomfortable with the idea of sin. I have seen sin used as a billy club to batter the proud into submission. The church is regularly mocked for publicly naming sin in the public forum. The word "sin" has even been reduced to silli-

ness in some circles, something used only by the most ignorant preachers.

Consider how you have responded to sin. Remember
what brought healing to those places where relationships
have been broken. Identify what repentance has meant. Look
for examples of whole groups of people repenting of their
involvement in societal sin. Bring knowledge of your own
past sins before God for guidance and new insight.

And then, consider also what response to the sins of white
privilege and internalized racist superiority might entail.
Look with new intensity at the prospect of repentance for
self-perpetuated ignorance, systemically pervasive uplift,
ingrained assurance of superiority. In the midst of these pon-
derings, remember also that God loves us. No matter what
we chose to do or what response may come about, God loves
us all the time. We cannot give in to loathing.

A final query

What does a healthy white person look like? Spend time
examining yourself as a white person who benefits from the
ongoing realities of racism's systemic misuse of power.
Identify where new knowledge burns like cleansing fire,
resounds like a crystal bell, or jolts us like a spark of recognition. Allow the Spirit to work through this examination to
raise new awareness of what becoming white twice might
mean, and how health might be brought about.

I know that I feel most healthy when I am brought before
the reality of racism without flinching, respond as I am able
to, and resist the arrogant belief that what I do will result in
final change. I know that my health as a white person has as
much to do with recognizing that I do not have all the
answers as it does with the specific actions I take.

A healthy white person understands her penchant for isolation, but she is actively engaged in antiracist action whether
in the home, at church, school, or workplace. A healthy white
person knows he likes being in control and that it will be
offered to him, but he is discovering grounding in God's con-

trol. The healthy white person realizes that she has lost much in the process of becoming white, but has begun the task of shaping a new identity not based on power and privilege. The healthy white person knows the ways in which racism has shaped him and continues to shape him, but he refuses to have that be all there is to him. The healthy white person does not pretend she is a person of color, nor does she make white people her enemy. He does not back away from the truth that shines within him. She is accountable for her actions to people of color, but she has not placed resistance to racism as the idol upon which all self-worth is determined.

There are many more questions to be asked and mused over. Take these as a place to start. The chapter that follows will now turn to asking the question, "How does whiteness hurt us?"

Ideas for action:

- Create a skit based on Mark 12:18-34 reading it as an encounter with internalized superiority.
- Take up Thandeka's challenge (see footnote 3) and describe yourself as a white person and use white references for a week.
- Make a chart of the four white spaces as described in this chapter. Add new tasks in each white space along with the primary tasks identified in this chapter.

8

How Does Whiteness Hurt Us?

You desire truth in the inward being; therefore teach me wisdom in my secret heart.
(Psalm 51:6 NRSV)

Tears and dancing

In preparation for attending a worldwide gathering of Christian indigenous peoples, Iris de León-Hartshorn, co-author of this book, shared with me a video of a previous conference. One Friday night, I turned on the VCR because Iris had assured me that I would be moved by what I saw.

She was right.

The video was filled with images of worship. But it was worship unlike any I had ever experienced. Group after group sang, danced, walked, chanted, and moved in their indigenous dress, language, and worship form. Jesus was clearly at the center of every expression of worship. I saw Maori, Choctaw, Filipino, Finn, and Zulu worship styles explode with jubilation.

One image penetrated the emotional screen I put up when Iris told me that I'd be moved. A middle-aged Indonesian man danced slowly across the screen with a power and grace I have rarely witnessed. As I watched him act out a battle with Satan, face filled with dignity and strength, I began to cry.

I cried for joy that this fully human, profoundly fleshy expression of worship was still with us. But I also cried out of grief that somewhere in the history of becoming white my own indigenous roots and identity had been left behind. I cried that my mother had been taught that dancing was a profound sin. So profound a sin that the church told her she could not be in the same room where it was taking place; even if that meant sitting by herself in a separate room while her friends' party went on without her. I cried that in my own congregation we barely register that we have bodies below our mouths.

I was reminded of a Sunday worship service in Chicago where Mennonites and Brethren in Christ had gathered to resist racism. On that snowy morning in March of 1995 we danced and worshiped. I cried there too. That time, though, I cried out of joy that white people and people of color had found a way, however haltingly, to dance and call God good.

Both of those events, the video of indigenous peoples and the Chicago worship service, placed before me all the evidence I will ever need that we who are white have lost something in the process of becoming white. As we have called ourselves white and declared ourselves superior, we have also become poorer. If nothing else, many of us have lost a vehicle for worship. We have lost touch with our bodies.

Tracing the spaces

The four white spaces I introduced in the last chapter, isolation, control, loss, and loathing, cannot be fully understood without some mention, however brief, of the historical forces that created white people. The formation of each space can be traced back to a time when choices were being made among European peoples to become something that they had not been before. In so doing they became white and chose a path of destruction that many of us yet walk on today.[1]

Isolation in history

One source of isolation, this penchant to deny a collective white identity, can be traced back to the destruction in Europe of many communal bonds during the slave societies of Greece and Rome.[2] Regardless of its original source, this latent individualism was refined and made grosser through forces found in the New World.

Follow the thought of the day, however irrational: Individuals own things. Things are sometimes people, especially if they look different than the English ideal. Individuals can own people. With this consciousness as a base, slavery, already practiced in Spain, Portugal, and some parts of Africa, took on a more heinous form. Pursuit of profit, racial hatred, and the twin innovations of lifelong servitude and inherited slave status, amplified an already corrupt institution.

Native peoples, well versed in communal practice and identity, resisted enslavement, but fell under a policy of removal and extermination. Where that did not work, the Dawes Severalty Act of 1887 intentionally sought to break up lands held in common by Aboriginal nations, thereby allowing for the purchase of that land by white individual landowners. Reservation land declined from 138 million acres in 1887 to 78 million in 1900.[3]

In all these efforts, white ideology proclaimed publicly and boldly what it had come to do. Theodore Roosevelt, referring openly to the "white" or "English" race, wrote, "There have been many other races that at one time or another had their great periods of race expansion . . . but there has never been another whose expansion has been either so broad or so rapid...."[4] Later on, the assumption of white supremacy had become so widely accepted and considered normal that white racial self-congratulation became unnecessary, and eventually was relegated to the margins of now vilified fringe groups like the Aryan Nations, Christian Identity Movement, or skinheads.

Ultimately, we arrive in the white space of isolation. So assumed is the supremacy of whiteness, so ingrained is it in society around us, that it is not necessary to speak its name. Once not spoken, it quickly (by white people only) becomes forgotten. We become isolated, refusing to acknowledge our group identity.

And then there is fear

In the midst of that isolation, I wonder about growing fears. Is it that despite all our privileges as white people, we still ultimately fear being exposed? Do we fear discovering that we are not as superior as we had thought?

A recent Website listing of readers' reviews of *Lies My Teacher Told Me* by James W. Loewen exhibits the fear growing out of isolation. While many reviewers praised Loewen's exposure of the nation-worshiping mythology of public school history books, a number did not. To be clear, I do not know the race of those who opposed his writing, yet one reviewer wrote, "He goes on and on about how bad anyone who has managed to do something with their life should feel [that person could only be a white male according to Loewen]."[5]

The latent vitriol evidenced in this statement seems to stem from the white fear of exposure that I attempt to describe here. What does happen to white people in general and white males in particular, when "success" is exposed as the legacy of white privilege? How does that affect our self-esteem? The legacy of racism provides a self-concept based on mendacious standards of merit, achievement, and potential. The exposure of such systemic falsehood can leave us shattered.

I wonder if we also fear losing our footing. If we have known only the feel of power and privilege beneath us, do we fear we will be unable to walk if that foundation is swept away? I remember a Good Friday evening in southern Lancaster County, Pennsylvania, while I was on spring break from college. Suddenly the earth moved. At first mistaking this minor earthquake for a malfunctioning furnace, my hosts and I scattered into the four corners of the basement. Uncertain of what to do next, we stood there long after the shaking subsided.

I was shocked to discover that a normally inactive fault line ran through that part of the county. My concept of the world around me dramatically shifted. For weeks after I told this story again and again. The foundation beneath me had only changed slightly, but I was afraid.

If this story holds truth for white people, then I think we will have a hard time walking should our efforts to dismantle racism actually bear measurable results. We will need to learn a new skill: how to walk without power and privilege leveling the path beneath us. I have no doubt that our sisters and brothers of color have much to teach us in this regard.

Control and history

Control and isolation trace many of the same historical outlines, but control is even more focused. Like the profit-based slavery system, the spirit of conquering and owning warps basic Christian tenets that would otherwise call the entire institution of slavery into question. Debates in many mainline denominations center on the distinctions between "free" souls and "enslaved" souls, not on the enslavement of white people to the oppressive spirit of racism.

Here we must also name those roots of the space of control in the capitalistic system itself. The profits gained from slave trade and labor fueled expansion in Britain and throughout the United States. Likewise the annexation of Mexico, the use of Chinese labor, and the ongoing appropriation of Native lands, added huge natural, human, and financial resources to the United States government and the white businessmen who supported it.[6] Throughout, white people remained in control.

Profit strode hand-in-hand with whiteness across the continent. Together they left behind whatever vestiges of spirituality that might have held them in check. The white space of control opened wide.

Physiology is clear; unused muscles atrophy. If the analogy holds, there is learning here for our spirituality in the white space of control. I know that I have become dependent on the privileges and control that I receive as a white person. As a result some measure of my spiritual "muscle" has atrophied. In short, I have not learned to be dependent on the providence and grace that God affords.

Whether using the image of health, muscle strength, or barrier between self and Creator, the receipt of white control adversely affects our spiritual growth and maturity. Racism as expressed in internalized racist superiority tries to set itself up as God, as the provider and maintainer of our every need. I believe that counts in some dangerously subtle way as its own immobilizing idolatry.

I do not think it is by accident that dependence on God's providence and warnings against idolatry are so closely linked in the Old Testament. Exodus 20:2-3 makes this linkage most plain as the first commandment is articulated: "I am the Lord your God, who brought you out of the land of Egypt, out of the house of slavery; you shall have no other gods before me." Inasmuch that racism succeeds in creating systems and institutions that provide control and privilege for white people, we who are white are constantly tempted to believe that racism is our provider. The minute that belief is internalized, we have set up a new idol. We forget who really provides for us. Racism wins.

History and loss

Loss stems from the very specific process of European groups being allowed to become white over against the people of color groups who were not. We cannot understand one process without being aware of the other. Already in 1671, "the British began encouraging the naturalization of Scots, Welsh, and Iris to enjoy all such liberties, priviledges [sic], immunities whatsoever, as a natural borne Englishman."[7] By contrast, it was not until 1952 that people of every race could be naturalized as a United States citizen.[8]

Suffice it to say that in the process of leaving behind language, dress, celebration, food, music, even family structures, in order to become white, other less obvious things were also lost. Traditions of resistance to oppression, expressions of spirituality, worldview, and connection with history—these too were lost.

Jeannie Romero Talbert, a colleague and friend, noted the many white volunteers in church organizations have worked hard to learn a language like Spanish. "But," she queried "Why don't they know the language of their own people?" I listened with particularly close attention. I can stumble my way through a conversation in Spanish, but know only a few words of my mother's first language, Pennsylvania Dutch. I, too, have lost something.

White loss and becoming black

One of racism's harsh paradoxes is that white folks have tried to become black in various times and places even after having declared that blackness is worthless. I was surprised to see recognition of this paradox on a network television show. A detective on "Law and Order: Special Victims Unit" offered the following rejoinder to a white teenager dressed in baggy pants and wearing a baseball cap backwards: "You could at least stop appropriating black culture for your own bad white self." The detective then turns the teenager's hat around and stomps off.

Donelda Cook refers to one manifestation of this paradox when she writes, "There has been a pattern in American society, as exemplified in the popular music industry, of whites initially devaluing aspects of black culture only to rename it and claim it as their own at a later date."[9] This took the specific form of white artists "covering" a song written and first performed by black artists. The song was reissued and widely distributed by white-owned companies. White producers and performers made lots of money while artists of color were left in the lurch.[10]

A number of years ago I was disturbed to discover that the private elementary school where my mother was principal was going to hold a "whigger" day. This almost exclusively white, rural school was going to encourage their students to wear baggy pants. I then told Mom where the term "whigger" came from (a combination of "white" and a powerfully offensive racial slur). The name of the day was changed but to my knowledge the dress patterns were not. The white students at this Christian school were ignorant of the meaning of the term. They knew even less about their whiteness or the appropriation of black culture, but the evidence was real, pervasive, and sad to see.

Whether acknowledged or denied, conscious or unconscious, singular or collective, the vacuum created by whiteness draws whatever it can unto itself. Whiteness does not care if those things taken in have been acknowledged or used with or without permission. In our collective rush to gain the glittering privileges that racism offered those of us of European heritage, we jettisoned the strength and sustenance that culture provides. Out went language, distinctive dress, and all but the barest bones of custom, history, and celebration. In return we became white and basked in whatever sense of superiority that brought us.

Should the students so ready to dress like a "whigger" be held responsible for their action? Do they understand what they have lost? Ten- and eleven-year-old girls and boys cannot be held responsible for the broad forces of history and specific parental choice that brought them where they are. But should they be challenged to create something new that does not require stealing from others? Likewise, while they could live their lives without being aware of having been, in the words of Tim Wise, "sucker-punched by racist conditioning,"[11] they cannot be unaffected by it.

History and loathing

I'll close this reflection on the historical sources of becoming white, by simply noting a primary source of the space of loathing. To become white we had to engage in the wholesale oppression of one group and the attempted genocide of another. No wonder we carry a residual realization that there is something inherent to our whiteness that cannot love itself completely. Whiteness was born out of oppressing others.

And so we sometimes show our commitment to antiracism by judging other white people as harshly as possible.

Clearly, it is difficult, uncomfortable work to name racism, its shape, entanglement, and evil. At times people will feel hurt through the process of exposing privilege and accommodation to evil. Yet, we must call our white brothers and sisters to new knowledge. We must feel together the loss of some of the best of who we could have been as we exchanged European culture and identity for becoming white. We can find a way to move beyond loathing.

But this is gravely different than exposing the racism of white people and then parading their sin. It is not the same as declaring racism rampant and then grinning as my white sisters and brothers squirm. Loathing leads to bashing white people over the head with truth until they are left dazed and bleeding on the floor.

Loathing expressed in this form ends up isolating white antiracists from potential allies in the white community. I remember an initial conversation with a group of white antiracist activists known for their clarity and courage. As I sat with them, I was able to name how intimidated I was by the level of experience and analysis in the room. I remember feeling afraid that I would be judged for not being sufficiently antiracist. I had witnessed some of their number bitterly denounce other white people for a lack of commitment.

Our ensuing conversation opened the way for me to feel more at home with this group of people. To date, I count a number of them among the most important of my mentors and co-strugglers. I know, however, that many of them, like myself, struggle to find ways to connect with all our white sisters and brothers and to do so without loathing.

Shame goes first

Describing the history and shape of these four white spaces can leave those of us who are white feeling immobilized. I'll note here the difference between shame, that can leave us immobilized, and guilt that can lead to action. The first holds the seeds of further destruction. The second points us toward the kingdom.

Shame paralyzes us by sending the message, "I am wrong and have no value."[12] As Meck Groot noted, "As white people, we have been given a legacy in which, though we are surrounded by people like us, we do not feel a connection to them. We are isolated and alienated little selves. On our own. Forced to be self-reliant or perish. This is why many of us are drawn to the communities of people of color."[13]

Groot's description of the white space of isolation is the primary breeding ground for self-defeating shame Tim Wise described. Although he used the word guilt, I think that shame can be inserted here meaningfully:

> Our guilt [read shame] is worthless, although far from meaningless. It has plenty of meaning: it means we aren't likely to do a damned thing constructive to end the system which took us in, conned us, and stole part of our humanity. [What is needed] is to end this vicious system of racial caste. For us to spend every day resisting the temptations of advantage, which ultimately weaken the communities on which we all depend.[14]

But shame is different than guilt. Guilt says, "I or we have done wrong and must change/repair."[15] As one workshop participant cautioned us, "Don't be too hard on guilt. It holds promise."[16] In the Christian faith, there is a strong tradition of guilt for sin leading to renewal, right action, and renewed relationship.

When guilt springs from clear-eyed assessment of the way things are, it transplants shame. When we as white people understand the white spaces racism creates, we will be able to respond with renewed, focused energy to join those movements working to dismantle racism.

Yelling at myself

Standing powerless before our personal compulsions, in need of God's providence and sustenance above all else, is at the heart of a mature spirituality. I have begun to recognize how powerless I am to stop myself from those compulsions that lie at the core of my being. Even though I deeply desire to be a loving parent every hour of every day, all too often my sons bear the brunt of a sharp word or uncommon impatience.

One particularly grumpy morning I asked Zachary if he was bothered by my ill-temper. When asked whether I should continue to be short with him, Dylan, or Cheryl, he vigorously shook his head no. However, he mischievously, but with true conviction, nodded in affirmation to my suggestion that perhaps I should yell at myself.

This personal story spells out a process that is also evident systemically. Just as individuals need to stand before God in humble recognition of continuing sinfulness, so too do groups need to recognize our collective helplessness to be rid of aggregate patterns of brokenness. A healthy guilt, whether individual or collective, can move us from self dependence to a dependence on God's providence.

Except in brief mockery, I did not yell at myself on that grumpy morning. I did, however, confess to Cheryl, my spiritual director, and to God my inability to do what I wanted. I long for the day when we as white people of faith can together confess our inability to remove ourselves from the clutches of racism. That confession will need to be offered first of all to God but then also to the communities of color that can hold us accountable and call us beyond safe acquiescence to our accommodation. I believe that the Spirit will then give us the power to act in ways as yet unimaginable. When that happens, antiracist values (and all principles that call us to life in Christ and away from death in the world) will be as regular as breathing.

Ideas for action:

- In a study session reflect on these questions:

   Isolation: In what ways is it possible to begin the task of acknowledging your membership in a group of people shaped into being white? Ask how many white people identify themselves as "white people." Where that has happened, what does it feel like? Write a list of all the times people remember having been identified by race. What were the experiences like? Contrast experiences of people of color as appropriate.

   Control: What has been the spiritual impact of being taught to control, being given control, or taking control? Is it possible to feel as if you personally have little control, but still be a member of a group that has lots of control? What biblical figures had to struggle with being put in control? What did it do to them (e.g., Joseph in Egypt)?

   Loss: What have you lost to become white? Can you name anything that you don't have and you might if your group had not become white? What has the collective lost? Do you even know where to start looking for what you've lost?

   Loathing: What kind of guilt visits you? Does it move you to self-love and love of your people? Have you seen others engaging in loathing around you? Where does that loathing come from?

- Write journal entries cataloging what you as an individual white person have lost because of being white. Add what white people as a group have lost.

- Organize an effort to include historical readings and analysis of whiteness from an antiracist perspective in your local high school curriculum. Use *Lies My Teacher Told Me* by James W. Loewen (Touchstone, 1996) as a resource.

- Write letters of protest to white-owned and controlled companies that are using other culture's music, style, and presence for financial gain: for example, Taco Bell's "South of the Border" theme and racially offensive Chihuahua advertisements, KFC's use of black culture in advertisements ("Go Colonel, Go Colonel"), etc.

9

How Do We Respond?

After this he went out and saw a tax collector named Levi, sitting in the tax booth; and he said to him, "Follow me."
(Luke 5:27 NRSV)

I often struggle with what it means to be white and work to dismantle racism. Once, while in the midst of a painful conflict, I told my friend Brenda, "No matter how perceptive the analysis, how courageous the stance, or how accountable to people of color, it is not right to bludgeon white people with an analysis of racism." I left that conversation longing for a way for white people, and particularly white males, to enter the work of dismantling racism and not screw it up.

And so I went back to the four white spaces racism gives us to look again at the tasks and values we can claim as we seek a way to enter the kingdom. I hope they also have something to say about how we who are white can enter the work of antiracism without messing up.

Isolation and the task of connecting

For me, one of the forms isolation takes is that I try to establish myself as a well-read, irreproachable antiracist expert. "Unlike other white people," I rationalize, "I have earned the right to no longer acknowledge the effects and reality of racism within me."

I recognize this incipient and slippery danger only because it has visited me so often. In one workshop, a white female participant expressed significant knowledge of a topic area in which I was presenting. Instead of welcoming her insight, I mockingly asked if she would like to teach the group. *She has no right to be the exception. That is my territory,* I said to myself. Fortunately another white male confronted me about what I had done.

Instead of isolation and exception, I've begun to identify with white resistance. When I say that racism makes all white people into racists, I try to put myself in the place of someone hearing those words for the first time. I then remember the resistance I originally felt.

It is the same resistance I feel when one of my colleagues of color challenges me about something I said. It is the same resistance I feel when I discover that I respond differently to the young Latino man walking in front of me on the sidewalk than I do to the young white man only a few blocks ahead of him.

Dody Matthias used the image of birthing. She once told me, "We have to remember the pain and discomfort we all go through as white people when we first become aware of racism's affects on us. It is like remembering the pain of coming out of the birth canal to look around at a new world."

I am not here talking about paternalistic condescension. I am talking about remembering how racism works to create racists of all white people. That it seeks to do the same to me. That I am yet in the process of coming out of the birth canal.

When I am able to connect with how difficult it is for all of us who are white to name our racism, I am better able to respond to resistance in a workshop. I am better able to talk without shame about antiracism in my majority white congregation. I am ready to stop protecting white people from the pain of facing our complicity in this racist system.

I am reminded of a passage in Luke where Jesus calls out Levi the tax collector (Luke 5:27-32). Not only does Levi follow Jesus, leaving everything behind him, but he then goes and brings Jesus to others like him. I see myself in Levi, someone who has gained much by cooperation with a system based on the oppression and distress of others. Like Levi, however, Jesus calls me to a new identity and asks that I connect with others like me.

I pray for the eyes to see white people in that crowd of "tax collectors and others" reclining with Jesus at Levi's house. I pray to acknowledge I am also at Levi's house. I end up also connecting with myself.

Control and the task of letting go

To state again what we said before, we who are white have been taught to expect to be in control. Like the Scribe who has become all too used to the best places at the table,[1] we do not want to let go.

In institutional settings, the desire for control takes the form of maintaining and promoting programs that are designed for the benefit of white people at the expense of people of color. Many of the short-term service ventures prevalent in many church mission agencies are a prime example of the unspoken desire of those institutions to stay in control.

Speaking from his experience as a young African-American recipient of short-term service, James Logan pointed out, "They were similar to study tours. I call them 'get-to-know-the-ghetto tours'. . . . Short, sound-bite service contributes to the destabilization of community. In that sense, short-term service is, I think, very much like crack cocaine and alcoholism; it gives a false sense of security. But it does not build a coherent, intergenerational community that empowers its members."[2]

Even in the face of this kind of evidence, the short-term service endeavor continues full-speed ahead. While admittedly complex and amorphous in administration and impact, the patterns of funding and participation that allow them to continue with such vigor seem to indicate that something else is going on. The fact that this form of service continues, even when that service may be harmful, speaks powerfully of the need for those sponsoring institutions to be controlled by white people.

The principal task I've identified in this white space of control is letting go. One concrete expression of that general principle is the idea of accountability to communities of color. Such accountability can put us in a place of not being able to rely on our white privileges.

When discussing the idea of accountability, the executive director of a large mission agency declared, "I don't know all that it means, but I do know it doesn't mean just letting people of color tell me what to do." At one level she was exactly right. The work of antiracism should never mean that any of us simply let go of our powers of discernment and willingness to listen to the Holy Spirit. However, a reluctance to be held accountable by people of color can also express itself as passive resistance with the end result being that control stays in the hands of white people.

A general value that we have sought to embody in our working relationship as a training team is that people of color get veto power. Upon occasion we do find ourselves at an impasse. If we simply cannot decide whether it is better to directly confront an uncooperative participant or let it go for the time being, we aim to give the people of color in the discussion the final say. If we are divided over a proposal to expose the actions of an overtly hostile administrator, again the final word goes to the people of color. In disagreements over training in potentially volatile settings, again the veto power is present.

Even though I resist being put in a place where I cannot depend only on my white control and privilege, I know how powerfully God can act when we allow ourselves to be grounded there.

A naming story

One example of accountability as an expression of spiritual grounding began after I had gone through a vision-initiated process of changing my name from Jody to Tobin. People of color who hold me accountable for my antiracism work called me to take on this new name. I took the name as a reminder of putting God at the center of the work of dismantling racism, not the anger and frustration that had been so clearly present before. Once the naming ceremony was complete, I assumed my learning was done.

A second vision pulled me way out of my comfort zone. I received instruction that I should, among other tasks, change my name legally, but not use any of our funds to pay for it. A few days later a lawyer agreed upon a deadline for the payment of the first half of the fee. I continued praying that I had heard God correctly, that the money would come, that God would make it happen.

When things didn't happen as I thought they should, I even placed an empty envelope in the lawyers' door one morning thinking that the money might magically appear by the time he opened it. It hadn't.

The day before the money was due I went to a trusted friend, Zulma Prieto, and asked her to pray that I would know what to do. The next morning she felt directed by the Spirit to tell me to stop saying I could pay the legal bill out of my funds. Instead, I was to boldly declare that God would bring the money by the end of the day.

During that morning's worship, I haltingly said that God would bring the money. I had been so conditioned, so protected from having to rely on God, that I didn't know quite how to step forward without the safety net of white privileges beneath me.

Even though I had named no dollar amount to anyone present, by noon the exact amount of the legal fee, $350.00, was handed to me in an envelope. When the second payment was due several months later the pastor of an African-American Mennonite congregation in California quietly told me that their congregation was going to pay the rest of the bill.

In this instance, I was put in a place where my white privilege and control could not help me. I simply had to be open to the Spirit's leading, to trust those holding me accountable, to go to a place to where I had not been before. In so doing, God's control was made clear to all of us.

Loss and the task of reclaiming

We who are white are seldom given the permission to grieve what we have lost. As an initial act of reclaiming who we can be when racism does not define us, we must grieve. Grieving allows us to hear what we have previously ignored and perhaps found too painful to respond in any way but that of intellectual pursuit. Lillian Roybal Rose described this hesitancy to grieve:

> If white people only confront those issues on a cognitive basis, they will wind up as hostages to political correctness. They will be careful about what they say, but their actions will be rigid and self-conscious. When the process is emotional as well as cognitive, the state of being an ally becomes a matter of reclaiming one's own humanity. Then there is no fear, because there is no image to tear down, no posture to correct. The movement to a global, ethnic point of view requires tremendous grieving. I encourage white people not to shrink from the emotional content of this process.[3]

I suspect that beneath much of our hesitancy to grieve is an emotional response begging to be expressed. Perhaps first in anger, maybe in denial, possibly even in weeping. All these are expressions of grieving the loss of our critical, life-giving parts of our humanity. It takes great courage and commitment to grieve.

Here again the importance of caring, nurturing communities where we can grieve the loss of our worldview cannot be underestimated. Without them, the possibility of moving from grieving to reclamation will not happen.

The reclamation task, particularly as expressed in learning more about our family history, can be a joyful, life-giving task. It should not be confused, however, with some contemporary "white-identity" movements that are not tied to a clear, well-articulated understanding of racism as a provider of power and privilege for white people.

To have integrity as white people, we need to enter the task of reclamation with full knowledge of the white society that tries constantly to shape white people into racists. When that is clear, we can engage in reclaiming who we are as a profound act of resistance to racism.

Knowing how we became white

Knowing how we individually became white can open the door to understanding how we collectively became white. Although it was difficult, here is some of what I have remembered about my own journey into whiteness.

In elementary school, Mrs. Schaffer, Miss Best, and Mrs. Gingrich praised my style of stillness, calm, and suppression of emotion. In fourth grade, Mr. Stump told us he longed for the good old days when his class, now predominantly African-American, had been white.

In fifth grade, I remember the day when Mr. Burger told us something was stolen from his desk and no one would leave until someone confessed. Two minutes later he left me, the only white boy in the class, go home because he "knew I wouldn't steal it."

In high school, Paul Lott, an African-American who was a preacher's kid like me, was accepted into the small circle of overachieving white friends I hung out with. Paul conformed, unlike Ray, who was also black but didn't mind letting us know.

When our son Dylan was in kindergarten, he came home from school and asked, "Daddy, why would our teacher say that I and [three other children] raise the class?" He had just named the four children of white parents in his kindergarten class. As I saw my son becoming white, I had to grieve. I also had to talk to him about what had taken place. We have much to reclaim together.

Loathing and the task of loving

Sometimes white people working to dismantle racism try to express their rock bottom commitment to the cause by lashing out at other white people. I do not believe that this is healthy or, in the end, works to dismantle racism.

Strangely enough, once we are aware of and committed to dismantling racism we who are white can sometimes feel more comfortable and at home with people of color than with other white folks also trying to dismantle racism. This has taken the form of reluctance to gather in white caucuses. While I have been a part of many white caucuses in formal training settings, I have not yet been able to find a way to gather with other white people committed to antiracism on a regular basis.

I am aware of white caucus gatherings that have proven sustainable and effective: European Dissent in New Orleans, People Against Racism in Harrisburg, and white groups associated with Women's Theological Center in Boston. Writing out of the context of one of these groups, Becky Thompson noted, "Building alliances with white people is a key way to counter the isolation we have sometimes faced as white antiracist people. . . . Often, we are among the few white people who bring up issues of race, network effectively with people of color, and consider racial equality integral to our work and humanity."[4]

The question is not whether or not to caucus. As white people, most of us caucus on a regular and ongoing basis. The question is how will we focus our discussion. Many of us live and work in white caucuses all our lives. The difference in caucusing as white antiracists is that we are given an opportunity to focus our discussions as white people and be held accountable for what we do. Central to our ability to focus

our discussion and action is the ability to love others and ourselves as white people.

It may seem strange that a systemic analysis includes
attention to the interpersonal principle of loving one another.
They are not, however, contradictory. The work of dismantling systemic racism and building new institutions that are
not based on power and privilege for white people needs to
be infused and embraced by a deep love for and among all of
us who are working together. The work quickly becomes
warped if it involves white people who fundamentally do not
love themselves.

One of the impacts of racism on white people, an outcome
of our conditioning of racist superiority, is an infatuation
with our privileges whether expressed in material, ideologi-
cal, or spiritual terms. Infatuation, as we know, is not built on
genuine love. Genuine self-love pulls us away from love of
privilege and can lead to effective, long-term, sustainable
communities who resist racism.

Infatuation with privilege leads to fear that they will dis-
appear. Self-love welcomes their withdrawal because they
only serve to prop us up. Infatuation with privilege focuses
on hate groups as the cause of racism so as to avoid attention
to its more subtle forms. Self-love as white people draws us
toward such racist communities because we know that is not
us, but could be. Infatuation with privilege sucks us into
cycles of accumulation that end up cluttering our lives in a
thousand ways. Self-love as white people recognizes the bur-
dens such objects place on us and draws us toward a new
freedom which does not require a wealth of objects to "fit in."

In the white space of loathing, we need to call for much
love. In so doing, we move closer to the kingdom.

A family story
While I have often struggled with ways to love white people like myself, there have been a few times when God's
grace has empowered me to do just that. One of the privileges
racism provides is the privilege of being silent in the face of

racist action. As a white person, I have the option of simply not saying anything, of choosing not to name the racism as it occurs.

At a family reunion one summer, two family members sat down to present a skit. The spouse of one of the two actors explained that this was a skit about a pastor and a "colored man." After a few more comments she went on to point out again that this was the pastor and a "colored man." The skit proceeded from there to show a confused, illiterate racist stereotype of the "colored man," complete with Southern drawl.

After getting over the initial shock of it, both Cheryl and I left the room. We talked briefly amidst our tears and embarrassment and decided together that we needed to return and say something. Although it was one of those moments of being caught between utter dread and sheer terror, we both knew that to have any integrity in the lives we had chosen to lead we needed to go back in the room.

And so, wishing that I would have just stopped and interrupted the skit to begin with, I did go back in and talk to the room of about 100 relatives about the pain that the skit caused us. I spoke with them about how much I wanted to be proud of my family. I described how disappointed and hurt I was by our collective silence in the face of that racist skit. I was glad that my boys could be there to see at least one small way of trying to love white people in the face of our racism.

Of course there is more to the story. I was so overcome with emotion after I spoke that I had to again leave the room to go outside and cry. Reentering the building the second time was even more difficult, but as I started in I was greeted by several relatives who wanted to be sure I knew how much they appreciated what Cheryl and I had been able to do. Their presence and support gave me the courage to go back into a space I did not want to enter and talk with folks I did not wish to see.

Enter the kingdom

I began these three chapters by trying to imagine what it would have been like for the scribe to hear Jesus tell him, "You are not far from the kingdom." I've wondered whether these four white spaces of isolation, control, loss, and loathing may be some of the things that block our complete entrance into the kingdom. I can only surmise that connection, grounding, reclaiming, and loving will remove those blocks specific to white people.

I do know that racism is a demon. I know that as a principality and power, racism seeks to keep us out of the kingdom. I know that God is constantly calling us to enter in, to move past those barriers, and find ways to be God's children that do not require a white identity empty of cultural strength, self-loathing, founded on control, and resulting in isolation.

Even as Iris and Regina have described the manifestations and effects of internalized racist oppression on people of color, these are the manifestations and effects of internalized racist superiority on white people. The superiority has become whiteness. I close, praying that God will show us a way to work with each other to become healthy white people and enter the kingdom rejoicing.

Ideas for action:

- Ask these questions in a study group:

   Isolation: What could connection look like in your life? In the life of your congregation?

   Control: What would it take for you to let go of control and be grounded in God's control? What would that take for your congregation or institution?

   Loss: What do you need to reclaim? How can your congregation support you in that task?

   Loathing: How can you love self, others, and your institution as white people?

- Create a grieving ritual to lament before God what racism has done to white people.
- Write down on a 3" x 5" card one way you can let go of

some control. Share cards with one other person. Check in one week to be held accountable for your action.

- Spend ten minutes talking with one other person about your experience of remembering when you became white. Don't be afraid of silence if it is difficult to remember experiences.

10

What Do People of Color Need from White Allies?

Two are better than one, because they have a good return
for their work:
If one falls down, his friend can help him up.
But pity the man who falls and has no one to help him up!
Also, if two lie down together, they will keep warm. But how
can one keep warm alone?
Though one may be overpowered, two can defend themselves.
A cord of three strands is not quickly broken.
(Ecclesiastes 4:9-12 NIV)

On needing something (Regina)

What do people of color need from white allies? From my observations, the question is either frighteningly difficult or deceptively easy for people of color to answer. The easy answers are often cynical: the best thing white people can do for me is (a) just leave me alone, (b) undo the past 500 years, or (c) try being me for just one day and see how far you get. Langston Hughes wrote a brilliant series of vignettes in which his alter ego, Jesse B. Simple, spends time on a bar stool ruminating over the facts of his life with a friend. The topic most often on his mind is race, and in one scenario Simple outlines what he wants from white people: a Game Preserve for Negroes. Having observed a nature reel in which vast areas of land are set aside to protect animals from harm by humans, he declares, "Congress ought to set aside some place where we can go and nobody can jump on us or beat us, neither lynch us nor Jim Crow us every day. Colored folks rate as much protection as a buffalo, or a deer."[1]

At the same time, the question is hard because at first glance, it seems to say things about the relationship between white people and people of color that are not true and don't sit well with us. It seems akin to the question, "Do you still beat your wife?"—there is no right answer. To confess need seems to admit that we are somehow lacking, admitting that white people have all the answers and the solutions to our problems.

But that is not what the question asks. The question presumes, as this entire book does, that all of creation is in relationship with one another. In any healthy relationship, there is giving and taking, each partner at times satisfying the needs of the other(s) to contribute to the all over well being of the whole. To be given something is not a bad thing, as long as the giving is reciprocal and the recipient has the option of saying what the need is. Too often people from the outside of our communities have decided what it is people of color need, and have done irreparable harm.

We think this is a fair question to ask.

And we seek a third way to answer the question, something that does not call for a return to segregation, nor a wish list of handouts. We seek a way to work together to emerge from the confines of racism's prison. The next several paragraphs offer suggestions of things individual white allies can do within personal relationships. The second half of this chapter speaks to systemic activity.

Know me. Get to know me as a flesh and blood person,

not a caricature. Don't base your understanding about people of color on what you see on television or in other media. We don't all look alike, speak the same language or dialect, think alike, or worship alike. Understand that my children are individuals as well. Work hard at undoing the stereotypes that you find present in your home, school, workplace, and church.

Honor my culture. Don't appropriate my cultural artifacts, style, and so forth without acknowledging the source, and then understanding the meaning of the object or the style. This means doing research. When you see something that comes from a people's heritage become a meaningless fashion trend or a moneymaking logo for a sports team, speak up. Let people know that many of these trends and styles actually dishonor the people they have come from. Tell why, tell how.

Value our artistic expressions. Quiz yourself right now— what do you think of when you hear the term "classical music" or "classical literature"? The most innocuous statements are sometimes laden with meaning. Traditionally, in this country we have considered real art to be European. Everything else is folk music and crafts and not really worth learning about.

In the same vein, it is time to teach *all* history. I laugh when I hear the argument that focusing on the histories of people of color is done to be politically correct and only serves to make children of color feel good about themselves. Isn't that what teaching white history has done all these years—make white children feel good about themselves? I once attended a Christian educator's retreat where I did a workshop on multicultural education in the church. During small group discussion time, I overheard a young white mother speak venomously about the fact that *Sesame Street* had started to teach a bit of Spanish and teach about various Spanish-speaking cultures. She argued that this was a waste of time for her children, because they had no need to speak Spanish. More terrible than her outrage to me was the fact that no one spoke up.

Appreciate our beauty. There is so much dis-ease in our communities revolving around white standards of beauty. Many of us are working hard to undo this. White people can support these efforts by not qualifying our dress, hair texture and styles, adornments, and so forth as inappropriate, weird, or distasteful. Many African-American women, myself included, have written and spoken about our hair issues. I am trying to raise my young daughter to appreciate the uniqueness and beauty of the hair God has given to her. It has happened that when combing her hair a. ound white people, someone will comment on what a tremendous amount of work it must be, or how they don't see how I put up with Rachel's hair, or similar comments. Or they will laugh about black people they have known and the funny things their hair does. These types of comments serve to emphasize the perceived "wrongness" of our hair, and feed into the myth that "good" hair is straight, "good" skin is light, and so on. Similarly, for white people who marry or adopt interracially, learn how to take care of your children's hair and skin. We do not use the same products and care techniques, and it is important for all children to learn to groom themselves properly.

Talk to your children, other family members and friends about the reality of racism. As the writer in Deuteronomy says about the Lord's commandments, talk about it "when you sit at home and when you walk along the road." That is to say, don't just wait until a horrific incident happens and you need to explain what happened, why, and how. Treat working against racism as you would any other justice issue, by examining the causes as well as the effects. There are age appropriate ways of introducing the issue to children as young as preschool. It is very tempting to tell our children God created us all equally and we should treat each other equally and leave it at that, but this does not prepare them for the real world they must live in. And it does nothing to counter the effects of the system of racism. They must know that although the above statement is true, many times in many places people have not lived that truth, and it is up to followers of Jesus to help bring about God's original intent for creation.

And especially for those working on behalf of the church and its institutions: **Think about me as part of your constituency,** not merely a specialized group. See me as a potential volunteer, employee, or funder—not only as an object of your mercy. Don't deprive me of the opportunity of ministering to you.

A systemic view (Iris)

Co-struggling is all about interdependency and finding ways, as people of color and white people, to get to justice. The survival of all creation has to do with interdependency, including the human race. And yet we have managed to separate ourselves from each other by race, gender, class, and many other ways.

Being open and vulnerable to see what we need as human beings can be very difficult. After being married for twenty-seven years, I finally understand that my husband cannot read my mind. When we were first married, I often would get frustrated with my husband because I felt he didn't understand me. I assumed he should just know how I felt or what I wanted. As a person of color I have also come to realize that the same trust and vulnerability must happen between white people and people of color in order to be co-strugglers on the issue of racism.

In order to know what we need to ask for, we need to know what we are seeking. As a person of color, I find this part very difficult. My experience has been that most white people say they are seeking racial reconciliation. I have personally struggled with this idea, that we can talk about reconciliation while knowing that racism continues in our churches, workplace, homes, and our society. Within a system as complex as racism, the injustice is many layered.

Maybe what we should be working toward in this struggle is "Restorative Justice" on a systemic scale. Working toward Restorative Justice, which would include dismantling racism, feels right to me. It's not going to be easy, yet, I believe that the struggle takes us where we need to go.

Up to this point primarily, Restorative Justice has been used for people who have committed a crime as defined by the legal system. Even though we may all agree that racism, in and of itself, is not a punishable crime, it is a violation against another person and group of people. One definition of crime is "an injury which violates person and community harmony."[2] I believe racism fits that definition because it is an injury that violates individual and community harmony on a daily basis in this country.

On accountability. For the most part, people of color do not want revenge, we want justice. To work toward justice, the first principle we need to live out is accountability. White people need to be accountable to people of color and work toward a fair process. Together we need to restore the community from the effects of racism. The principle of accountability asks us to focus on problem solving, liabilities, and obligations. It is not about turning the tables.

As people of color, we become frustrated and humiliated when we are not taken seriously about what we have experienced on both a personal and systemic level. When a principle of accountability is lived out, we are heard and our experiences are taken seriously as we develop a fair process together. When white people hold themselves accountable to people of color, we are no longer victims but people who have been wronged and are now being given a chance to speak, human being to human being.

Not about punishment. Restoring justice is not about punishment. It is not about retribution. At the same time, when white people take responsibility for their behavior and the systemic reality of racism they benefit from, some pain will be involved. The work of repairing the damage done by racism is painful. In order to be co-strugglers on this issue, people of color and white people must be willing to work toward restoration in a meaningful way for all. Our hope is that all people will be restored and treated with dignity.

One of the most tragic things about being human is desiring to hurt those who have hurt us. While most of us do not act them out, deep down inside most people have those feelings. Historically we have seen the oppressed become the oppressor and the oppressor, the oppressed. If we choose to look to punishment then we, as people of color, will exert what power we have to get even.

By using Restorative Justice as a way to restore our humanity toward each other, we can become a community of healing instead of a community of destruction. Jesus never sought to get even, but rather to restore people. In Mark 5:21-43, we see Jesus defying an unjust system by restoring two people caught in the midst of the purification system. Jesus' concern was not only to restore the individuals, but also to expose an unjust system.

Making it measurable. The third principle I want to introduce here is that reparation must be measurable. As mentioned earlier, accountability has to do with problem solving, liabilities, and obligations. This third principle takes it further in saying we must be able to measure how much reparation has been achieved.

As we measure reparation on a systemic level, we need to ask, "Are direct, identifiable shifts in the community taking place so that people can live healthy productive lives?" For the Native American community, reparation could revolve around land issues and/or employment opportunities. In Latino communities, we may need to include educational concerns. For example, are the barriers that have kept Latino children from succeeding at the same level as white children in the education system being removed? For other communities of color it may mean finding ways to remove toxic dumps and factories. In every instance, we need clearly identifiable indicators to measure the reparation process.

In our antiracism work, we encourage institutions to make one-, five-, and twenty-year plans. The specific goals set by the teams participating in our process provides one way to measure whether or not we are dismantling racism and bringing restoration to our institutions. If we are not intentional in our work against racism and toward restoration, it will never happen.

Defining victims and offenders. In a system based on Restorative Justice, offenders are defined by their behavior and their capacity to take responsibility, while victims are defined by their losses and their capacity to participate in the process of recovering losses as they move toward healing.[3] This is the place where we can work as co-strugglers against racism. As co-strugglers, we can find a way to work together to recover our mutual losses. In the end, racism harms both white and people of color. The question before us is, "Can we begin our healing together?"

I believe the description above of victims and offenders is accurate even when relating to racism. I also am aware that it is uncomfortable. Even though we do not want to define white people as criminals, their complicity with systemic racism has resulted in immoral and/or unethical behavior. Due to this recurring behavior, people of color have experienced losses on both individual and systemic levels.

Both individual and systemic. The fifth and final principle I want to introduce here involves both the individual and systemic dimensions of racism. On the systemic level, the larger community must be involved in addressing the conditions that allow racism to exist in our church, workplace, community, and homes. We must be committed to dismantling racism where we are and find ways to work together.

This means working for restoration on both individual and systemic levels. People of color also have responsibility to work toward their healing. We must be willing to enter into relationships with white people that will require us to speak honestly of the harm our communities have suffered, share our losses, and be able to work as co-strugglers.

Both people of color and white people are wounded, but in very different ways. In order to work with each other without our wounds getting in the way, we must work on our internalized racist oppression and internalized superiority. While working on those issues, we are then prepared to together dismantle racism by taking our perspective places within a Restorative Justice framework.

What Restorative Justice brings

I believe the Restorative Justice model has a lot to offer in the work of dismantling racism. To begin with, this model takes away the pressure from people of color to reconcile when they are not at a place to consider reconciliation. We are convinced that there be no reconciliation without justice.

Likewise, a Restorative Justice framework allows people of color to be involved in the restorative process. So many times a major institution, like the federal government, makes decisions on how to reverse harm done to a people without the people harmed being involved in the process.

The Restorative Justice model also enables white people to work at reparation issues instead of being immobilized by guilt. Many times I hear white people ask "What do you want from us?" or "What more do you want?" As hurtful as those questions may be for people of color, I can understand the frustration. Though I do not speak for all people of color, I believe many of us can say we want to be heard and we want restoration. The act of hearing and being heard begins the healing process for both whites and people of color.

Finally, a Restorative Justice model allows us to work together to address the conditions that allow racism to exist. No longer is it just an individual responsibility, but the community must become involved in dismantling racism.

Antiracism work needs to be in dialogue with people who work on Restorative Justice. Together we can find ways to further modify the principles identified here in ways that would speak even more clearly to the issue of racism. As I said earlier, the rush toward reconciliation makes me uneasy because something has been missing. I believe Restorative Justice helps identify those missing steps. With the addition of this framework, our journey becomes clearer and we are able to take one step at a time, allowing God to lead us to our homeland, the city of God.

I am hoping that the introduction of these Restorative Justice principles into the work of antiracism will be the beginning of a new discussion about finding helpful ways to be co-strugglers. Through this discussion, we can arrive at the even more important goal of the transformation for all people involved in dismantling racism. I'd like to invite white people into this dialogue. With God's help and grace, maybe we can find our way home together.

Ideas for action

1. Take the five Restorative Justice principles outlined in this chapter and identify specific examples of what those principles would look like if followed in your school, congregation, workplace, or institution. Which would be difficult to implement? Which would be easy?
2. Look at the suggestions for individual white action. Identify ways you know of that white people in your group have tried to implement them. What have the reactions been to those kinds of deeds? Have people responded negatively, positively, or indifferently?
3. The authors contend that it is a fair question to ask, "What do people of color need from white people?" Gauge levels of agreement and disagreement to the appropriateness of asking this question. How can a question like that move people forward to effective antiracist action?
4. On a chalkboard or piece of newsprint, write two columns, one headed by "Reconciliation" and one, by "Restorative Justice." Based on the information contained in this chapter and your collective knowledge of how those terms get used, identify similarities and differences. What are the relative strengths and weaknesses of the two concepts as they relate to the work of dismantling racism?
5. Practice short role-plays based upon the following scenarios referred to in this chapter. Upon completion, reflect on the ways in which practicing ahead of time prepares us to respond to racism whenever it is made visible.
   - During a study session, a member of a small group complains about Spanish words being taught on *Sesame Street*. How do you respond?
   - A member of your congregation displays an offensive

Native American caricature on their vehicle (such as Chief Yahoo of the Cleveland Indians). How do you respond?

- Your child comes home from school complaining about the classical literature course she needs to take next year. How do you respond?
- While a choir from an African-American congregation is visiting your white church, you overhear a co-congregant ask his spouse, "Do all of them have such kinky hair?" How do you respond?
- The chair of the mission commission at an all-white congregation of which you are a member proposes sending a work group to repair the sanctuary of a Latino congregation in a nearby city. How do you respond?

11

What White People Need from People of Color in Solidarity Relationships

And the Word became flesh and lived among us, and we have seen his glory, the glory as of a father's only son, full of grace and truth. (John 1:14 NRSV)

An innocent question

The question came about innocently enough. Regina, Iris, and I were sitting in a stuffy room in the Cleveland airport brainstorming about what shape the final "practical" chapters of our book should take. I think it was Iris who first articulated the questions we decided to ask of each other: What do people of color need from white people? What do white people need from people of color?

Intuiting that I needed others to think about this question with me, I soon sat down and wrote to twenty-two white women and men involved in the work of antiracism. Most of them belonged to teams active in the Damascus Road antiracism process for which Regina, Iris, and I provide leadership. After a short description of the book we were trying to write, I asked each of them this same question, "What do white people need from people of color?"

Replies quickly poured in and I immediately became aware that this was an important question to ask, if for no other reason than that the answers were so heartfelt and searching. Among these white organizers, activists, church leaders, and agency personnel, I heard a deep longing for authentic relationship.

"I need one person of color to be vulnerable with me," wrote Karen.[1] Bob raised the possibility of moving from "conversations and questions toward histories, spirituality, feelings, delights, loves, frustrations, children, hobbies, fears, goals. . . ."[2] Marty added with simple power, I need "to be able to rest with brothers and sisters of color as a sister."[3]

A gnawing edge

Those answers resonated with me and felt true, but I was yet left with a feeling of incompleteness, a dissonance, a gnawing edge. To add yet another metaphor, the longing for relationship was clear, but something hadn't yet come into focus.

Others added their insight. Ryan: "I want my friends to be willing to see the part of me that is struggling to change."[4] Sharon: "Your full partnership in the gospel of Jesus Christ."[5] Sylvia: "Let me be uncomfortable with my racism."[6] Phil listed the need for help in developing a more integrated spirituality.[7] Daryl asked for clarity of expectation.[8] Bob desired a safe place to be "vulnerable, white, confessional, ignorant, to ask dumb questions."[9] Karen asked to be "shown the way to get where I need to be going."[10] Everett's first response was "a shared analysis of racism" because he found it particularly

difficult when an analysis of systemic racism and white privilege is viewed by a person of color "as a threat to a white
person who is providing the person of color with patronage
and privilege."[11]

As I read the responses, I found myself agreeing with
some, shaking my head at others, feeling uncertain about a
few more. The truths I knew as bedrock were also reaffirmed.
On the centrality of white accountability to people of color
many respondents identified this as a given. Betty noted,
"We need to keep working at ways of carrying [accountabili-
ty] out, hearing other's experiences, and continuing to build
effective models."[12] Daryl described the need to be accountable to persons of color "who hold positions with equal or
more institutional power than my own."[13] Jeanne articulated
it this way, "I need . . . some direction in how to do something
that is not taking over or trying to be a 'fixer' or taking all the
power . . . [and] some accountability for that action."[14] Glenn
simply wrote that he needs heightened "expectations for my
actions and behaviors. I don't know how to ask for those
things, but I know I need them."[15]

None of the responses I've quoted here so far surprised
me. They represented the full range of responses among
white people struggling to live out an antiracist identity. In
every case, the respondents responded with all the honesty
and insight they had to offer. I was grateful to have been
reminded of truths I once knew and, in some cases, had forgotten.

An unexpected thread

Then I read the responses again. The second time through,
I noticed a thread I had missed before. In short, I had missed
testimonies about grace:

"As grace and as a key to a more whole and sane and life-
giving future."[16]

"Some words that come to mind: challenge, grace, hope
. . . ."[17]

"Probably it is like being willing to accept the grace of

God. Part of it is a feeling of unworthiness, but also it is coupled with a fear for what changes might be brought on as a
result of accepting that grace."[18]

Another, while not using the term "grace" specifically,
described the same. "It is not the responsibility of people of
color to be my friends. Relationships are a gift."[19]

Having noted this thread of grace, I began to understand
some of the gnawing edge I had earlier felt. But I still had not
fully understood it.

One of the responses I received answered my original
question, "What do we as white people need from people of
color?" with particular passion and insight. My friend and
co-struggler in the work of antiracism, Dody Matthias,
answered my question this way:

> So, I don't "expect" anything from People of Color. In
> other words, I do not want to lay my agenda/expecta-
> tions/needs on People of Color in any way that puts
> something on them to **do** or to **be** for me. "Expect" car-
> ries the connotation of the slave experience where white
> people always expected something quite unattainable
> from People of Color. It continues today when White peo-
> ple expect People of Color to explain, to teach, to per-
> form, to sing and dance. No—I humbly do not
> "expect/need" anything. Instead I prepare myself to
> respond to their agenda and to receive the gifts they are
> willing to share with me when—**in the course of their
> decision making** [my emphasis]—they find me ready to
> receive them. The one thing of which I am certain is that
> the moral leadership in the work of justice never comes
> from the perpetrators, but from the survivors. So, when I
> am ready to receive this gift, I have always found it to be
> extremely helpful. This is not to imply that I am self-suffi-
> cient. However, we're still not at a point where there can
> be mutual covenantal expectations between "equals" so
> long as the oppression continues.[20]

When I finished reading her note, it felt like I finally
understood what had been gnawing at me as I asked others

to respond to me. But I couldn't stop there. Now *I* had to answer the question.

My turn to answer

So now it is my turn. After having listed the responses, thoughts, and insights of many of those who wrote to me, I'll attempt to answer the same question I asked them: "What *do* I think white people need from people of color?" I'll boil it down to three statements. I write "statements" deliberately because I'm not sure they really are answers. They don't complete or summarize what others have written here already. They're not final (because I'm constantly being challenged in this area). And, as you'll see, they contradict each other. These are simply the best ways I know to respond to this question within the complexity of a thoroughly racist church and society.

The only thing I need is accountability. I write this first statement using the least nuanced meaning of the word "need." This need is a principled, clear, necessity to be accountable to the leadership of people of color for my antiracist work with white sisters and brothers. The need grows from a humble recognition that the greatest temptation I face is to give in to being normal, to fitting in, to being rocked to sleep by the incessant waves of racism. I need to be held accountable in whatever manner people of color themselves choose to hold me accountable. I cannot determine for them what that accountability will look like.

But the need for accountability also extends, in ever deeper and richer ways, to other white people calling me to listen to the whisper of the Spirit, to nudge me out of familiar paths, to let go of control when I can, and to name racism whenever I see it. This accountability to white people does not supplant that of people of color, it is much more the first level of checking, of interference if you will, where we challenge each other to take antiracist risks in appropriate ways.

The best way I know of to institute this accountability is for people of color always and in every setting to have veto power over white antiracist activity. The hardest thing I know to do is to simply take no for an answer. It is, I believe, one of the spiritual disciplines we who are white are called to live out.

The only thing I need is relationship. Already I am contradicting myself. Perhaps. Then again, perhaps not.

Here I use "need" in the sense of deepest desiring, of longing, of hoping that I might find myself in an authentic relationship with people of color. I desire for this to be true. I can work without that relationship present. I can name and struggle to dismantle racism by merely being held accountable for my actions, but on some core level that is not enough. The only thing I need (desire/long/hope for) is relationship.

But I must also be crystal clear that I could no easier demand trust and mutuality in a relationship with a person of color, than I could demand that God love me. The demand simply doesn't count. It is both so inconsequential as to be meaningless and so importunate as to be offensive.

For we who are white, relationships with people of color are a gift to be received. They come as gifts, often in the midst of struggle to dismantle racism, but they are not ours to ask for. They may very well be something we desire and need, but we cannot demand that they come about.

The willingness to be broken as white people in our desire for relationship with people of color and to accept that those relationships may or may not come into our lives is a second discipline I believe the Spirit has given us in response to this question.

The only thing I need is grace. This third need is the most dangerous to even write down. Too often, I have seen my white sisters and brothers jump to the need for grace without authentic struggle, engagement, and risk-taking. I have seen us look like pouty adolescents who have been confronted with their error only to whine that we've talked about it enough already and can't we get back to how things were before.

The "how-things-were-before" is racism. We cannot want to get back to it, jump over it, push it aside, underestimate it, ridicule, retrofit, or rely on it. We have to discover a way to want to get rid of it.

As I wrote earlier, I am convinced of the power of racism. I have seen how it works to create racists and victims. I know that this power and principality deals death and does it well. Racism is sin. This is true.

I am also convinced of God's power. I have seen God work to call out communities of resistance. I know that God deals life and does it abundantly. God is love. Grace tumbles down.

And time and again, counter to all reason, all history, all present practice, the instruments of that grace in the midst of racism are people of color. I need (am best served/called to transformation/humbled by) that grace because it is how I will learn to be defined by something other than race.

I can't make my privileges go away or even diminish them very much. I can't heal the legacy of racism by a single act of repentance. I can't put things aright even through an act of sacrificial giving or dramatic restoration (of land, property, financial resources). None of that will be sufficient. Most of those things will leave me in the seat of the giver, the controller, the one who has brought about the restoration.

Yet when I can learn to sit still and receive the grace that is offered to me in the midst of whatever actions I am taking, while waiting on God, while being open to not being in control, that is when we who are white might find a way forward. Can we receive the grace that people of color have to offer us? Learning how is the third spiritual discipline I think we white folk are called to engage in.

Truth and grace

The Gospel of John uses two powerful words to describe Jesus' mission: truth and grace. As I have struggled to understand myself and my role in the world, as a white person, a male, a Christian, and a child of God, those two words have come back to me time and again.

We all live in the midst of truth and grace. Racism works to hide and distort both. How wonderful it is when we see them without distortion.

Take the dream I had one night, for example. In the dream Cheryl was preparing to take a trip in a hot air balloon with Zachary and a friend of his from church. As she was stepping into the basket where the two boys already sat, something went awry and the balloon rose. Almost immediately the balloon was lost to our sight, so quickly did it sail away. I ran inside and dialed 911. The phone refused to work properly, I was put on hold, no one was able to help, and most refused even to hear my story. After several hours of struggling with a balky phone and receiving no help from the police, the local airport, even a vender of hot air balloon trips, I finally hung up. With the vision of these two young boys cowering in a fragile basket high in the air, I began to sob, helpless, unable to bring about their rescue. The dream ended.

It is a rich dream and, unlike most, I remember it in detail. In particular, the feeling of helplessness in the face of this impossible emergency stays with me. As of this writing, I do not know all the levels of meaning bound up symbolically in a balloon adrift and my frantic, failed attempt to save my son. But I do know that racism is an impossible emergency. I do know that my response, as someone who has been taught that I have the solution to others' problems, has been to frantically try to fix those around me and myself.

I work hard every week to make our antiracism training effective enough, our long-term planning insightful enough, and our risk-taking bold enough to bring an end to this demon, to bind it, kill it, and dispose of it forever. I strain and struggle to bring every area of my life in sync with my ideal of a perfect white antiracist. I demand that God act now, to stop allowing racism to murder, deform, and make miserable people of color while protecting the likes of me.

I have been taught to expect that my demands will be listened to, that my struggle will result in quick and smooth change, and that my plans will unfold as I want them to. But it does not happen. Not only is the phone balky, but someone who I thought was an ally publicly attacks my work, other friends and allies leave, some say that the institution I work for holds no hope of ever changing from anything but a racist club of well-intentioned white people. Things do not go as I plan. Like in the dream, I weep at my inability to bring about the change I seek.

Jacob's gift

Grace can and often does come in unexpected packages. One spring not so long ago, a young man by the name of Jacob Charlton[21] called me up to ask if I could talk with him. We found a time. As I hung up, I wondered what he was looking for.

Jacob was a recent high school graduate who had been a part of our congregation's youth group. Since his graduation we had kept in touch through a variety of work and social settings as he no longer attended our congregation. I enjoy Jacob and know him to be a diligent, creative seeker of truth and faith.

The gift of grace that Jacob gave me that day was the first of several he would give in the ensuing months. Jacob sought me out to simply talk through the racism he recognizes in himself. As we have talked, sometimes at our home or sometimes while driving around town together, he has expressed insight, challenged me about my racism, and identified actions he has decided to take.

During one of our conversations, Jacob shared with me a poem he had written about a walk he took on the way to our house one day. Using language too raw and real to quote at length here, Jacob described the interplay of the scenes around him with the thoughts he supposed were in the minds of the African-American and Latino people he passed along the way. His poem closes with this stanza:

At last, I arrive at my destination,
On the 600 block of South Lime,
I hope I can hide my anxiety
From the boys I'll be babysitting.
I go up the steps and ring the doorbell.
I am safe at last at my destination,
A white man's home.

Seldom have I been gifted with the promise of such honest, vulnerable searching. Jacob has demonstrated for me what we who are white need from each other. We need to be offering each other the truth of our own racism and the grace of encouraging each other to respond with passion and boldness. If we can learn to accept and open ourselves to the kind of grace Jacob has given to me, we will, I believe, be better prepared to receive the grace that people of color, as God's instruments, have to offer us.

Where this leaves us

Lastly, I wonder how the gift of grace calls us to action, to being, to a place where we do not have to depend on racism's privilege and assurance or superiority to survive. To a place where we know that the only thing we need is accountability, is relationship. Where we know we cannot bring either about.

Grace tumbles down all the time. A healthy white person rejoices when she is drenched with this gift from God.

Those are my responses today to the question that Iris and Regina originally asked me. They are not complete, final, or congruent. I offer thanks to all those other white people, co-strugglers every one, who shared their thoughts with me.

Ideas for action:

- In a study setting ask:

    How would you answer the question, "What do white people need from people of color?"

    Which of the answers quoted here make the most sense to you? Which raise more questions?

    Are Tobin's three answers (I only need accountability; I only need relationship; I only need grace) contradictory? If so, how? If not, why?

    How have you experienced God's grace? Is it reflected here in the discussion of the grace that people of color offer white people?

- Interview ten white people in your school or workplace

with the question, "What do white people need from people of color?" Compare your responses to those in this chapter.

- Improvise a meeting between three people, each of whom promotes one of the three answers the author proposes (accountability, relationship, grace). Look for new insights and learnings.
- Write poetry that explores the theme of white people accepting the leadership of people of color. Examine and express emotions related with the consideration or experience of this principle.

12

Missed Opportunities

Give instructions to the wise, and they will become wiser still; teach the righteous and they will gain in learning.
(Proverbs 9:9 NRSV)

Opportunities not taken

We have spent eleven chapters laying the theological and theoretical groundwork for white people and people of color working together to dismantle racism. We have journeyed through the different issues facing people of color and white people, examined what we need from each other, and placed all this thought thoroughly in the context of our Christian identity. It is time to get practical.

In the final two chapters of this book, we will share stories from our work together over the course of nearly seven years. In particular, this chapter will focus on those times and places where white people could have been allies for people of color, but were not. By doing so, we want to demonstrate the essential role white allies have to play as proactive risk-takers, able to follow the lead of people of color. Each story of an opportunity not taken will be followed by alternate endings consistent with antiracist principles.

In chapter 13 we will tell stories of what has worked well in the course of our struggle together. Even in the midst of recurring setbacks and ample mistakes, we have been given signs of hope again and again. We will share them in this last chapter not out of triumphant bravado, but as gifts that have been given to us in spite of our humanness.

Earlier in this book, Tobin identified the unnamed scribe as a white person "not far from the kingdom." In that story, Mark does not tell us how the scribe responds to Jesus' words. We know only that the scribe was presented with an opportunity to do something different, to not act in the way that other scribes were expected to act, to move beyond the privileges afforded him as a scribe. In the stories that follow, white people were also presented with an opportunity to do something different, to not act in the way that other white people were expected to act, to move beyond the privileges afforded them as white people. In these instances, they did not act as allies.

Told in both the first and third person, we have changed some details in many of the stories. Our desire is not to shame those involved. We offer these examples as a means to learn from others' mistakes so that they might not be repeated.

Conference call

The nine dim voices sounded particularly tinny on that October night. West Coast, East Coast, Midwest, and the South were each represented on the conference call. Gathered together at phones in homes and offices, the discussion focused on who the final candidates for the national executive director would be. No one could see anyone else, but furniture rustlings, dog barks, and other domestic sounds were intermittently audible in the background.

After opening prayer, the board chair invited an initial round of response to the document sent out ahead of time. Awkward silence followed. Finally one of the six board members on the call, all of whom were white, three women and three men, spoke in support of one candidate. Others followed. It quickly became evident that this one candidate was receiving a majority of the support.

Of the three staff members on the call, two of whom were women of color, the other a white male, all had participated in the discussion and had full voting status on the selection committee. The white male, Henry, had spoken around and about the emerging leader, but had not come out strongly in favor of the candidate. Maricella and Yvonne, the two staff of color, had proposed a second candidate they thought was equally strong.

Within minutes of Maricella and Yvonne each separately proposing this second candidate and explaining why both of them thought that person would do well as the executive director, the chair proposed that they only interview the first candidate "since this looks like our best option." Discussion continued by all the white members of the committee, but Henry noticed that Maricella and Yvonne had essentially dropped out of the conversation.

Without making any reference to the way in which their suggestions had essentially gone unacknowledged, Henry decided to again suggest the name of the same candidate that Maricella and Yvonne had previously put forward. He used the same reasons they had for supporting the candidate. Almost immediately, the other white members of the committee agreed to add the second candidate to the finalist list and thanked Henry for coming up with the idea. By the time the conference call ended, the committee had agreed to interview two candidates. Maricella and Yvonne had not said one word in the last forty-five minutes of the call.

The next day in the office Maricella and Yvonne sought out Henry to talk about the call. All three had worked together for some time and were close friends and leaders in efforts to dismantle racism in their organization. In a direct manner, they confronted Henry for how he had acted in the conference call. Henry had made the conscious choice to name and then take the credit for the idea originally put forward by

Maricella and Yvonne. He explained that he had noticed their silence and had wanted their idea to move forward. They responded that the racism had gone unchallenged and they had, once again, been rendered invisible.

What could have happened: In this story, I, Tobin, am Henry. As I am writing it, I remember again how I deliberately made a choice to take the less confrontational path even though I knew that racism was at work. If I had spoken my heart then and there, it would have required much less effort than did the following weeks of individual and corporate challenge to the rest of the board members for how we all had acted. Likewise, my actions put in jeopardy a relationship of trust between myself and Maricella and Yvonne.

I can imagine a different outcome than what happened here. I can imagine a different phone call where I had simply said, "Maricella and Yvonne have each proposed a candidate that we have all ignored. I'd like to suggest that we stop the process for a moment to decide together what that means." I don't for a second think that the responses by the other white members of the conference call would have been welcoming or inviting to such a proposal. But I do believe I would have been acting to name the racism that was among us rather than trying to cover it up.

Taking over

Because a person is committed to working against racism does not mean that racism stops affecting that person's life. It's devastatingly easy to fall back into old patterns of relating, to be pulled back into the box in which racism says we belong. Over the years this has become apparent even in the midst of doing antiracism work.

Early on in the history of Damascus Road, Tobin and I (Regina) were responsible for chairing a meeting together. This was a gathering of people in our network, folks who had gone through Damascus Road training. We had come together to get new information about resources and to plan some next steps for specific institutions and for the network as a whole. Tobin and I had worked together many times before and in fact, were close friends. I was certain then and remain certain now of his commitment to being an antiracist ally.

Toward the end of the gathering, something happened. Tobin and I had divided up the time so that we were each presenting to the entire group for an equal amount of time. I should mention that Tobin and I bring very different styles (part of what makes us a good team) to our working together. One of the ways this is evident when working with groups is that he thinks fast on his feet and is quick to answer questions. I take more time, often thinking my answer through before saying anything. I also may have more than one spin on the answer to a question, being hesitant to say I have "the" answer to a question or "the" solution to a problem.

In the midst of one of my presentations, Tobin answered a question from the sidelines where he was sitting. A few moments later, a question was directed to him. Slowly the room's attention began to shift from the front where I was supposedly leading the discussion to the side. Our roles shifted. Someone even attributed something I had said to Tobin.

This is one of those slippery areas were it's easy to say, "I don't see what the big deal is" or "You're being too sensitive." Some will want to argue as to whether this instance represents racism at all. After all, he didn't mean anything by it. In fact, the room was full of well-meaning people and the temptation was very strong for me to feel as if I was the one with the problem.

In reality, everyone in the room shared the problem. We had all been socialized to believe (even those of us who knew this was not the case) that white men have the answers, white men are the ones in charge, and white men are the ones to be listened to because white men know truth.

As a result of what was happening, instead of speaking up and taking charge, I helped my presence diminish. I shrank back, letting my disappointment and anger further silence me. I began to doubt whether I had anything important to contribute to this discussion, after all.

What could have happened: Tobin could have directed the group back to the front of the room by acknowledging that he was not presenting and that I was. He could have simply stopped answering questions. When a comment I made was attributed to him, he could have corrected the person. We both could have called attention to the dynamics in the room and named them as a manifestation of racism at work.

Of sweet grass and sage: a Midwest conflict

The next story brings such a level of complexity and struggle to it that we have decided to use it both in this chapter and the next. We will bring multiple perspectives to what we saw happening at this event since all of us were present. First, we'll present the basic details of the story. Then we'll reflect on some of the things we learned from the incident. In the following chapter, we'll return to the story with examples of how things went well.

A group of 50 Midwesterners have gathered together after a two-month break. Previously they had gone through a two -and-a-half-day antiracism analysis training in a different location. From the trainers' perspective, that particular analysis training had been marked by a higher degree of intensity than usual. Although it is not unusual for conflict to emerge, a small, but vocal group of participants had felt forced to participate and deeply mistrusted the training staff. From the onset, the trainers had been pegged as outsiders to the region.

The second application training got off to an equally conflictual start. Not only did several participant teams continue to mistrust the training staff, but inter-team animosities had begun to surface. Stemming from previous conflicts between church institutions in the region, a stranger walking into the room would have been able to immediately discern that the atmosphere was far from relaxed. Arms were held close, bodies were stiff, few smiles graced faces, and sentences were cropped and short.

After a supper break, the staff invited participants to talk informally with anyone they needed to in order to free them up for the work at hand. The group then broke into racial caucuses to look at and discuss the tensions in the room. Each caucus reported to the larger groups and teams spent a bit more time discussing if they were ready to move forward. Finally the group dismissed for the evening with plans to reconvene in the morning and attend to the work of dismantling racism.

In the main, the schedule proceeded as planned for the next two days. On the evening of the third day, the team planning the closing worship asked if anyone was allergic to sage or sweet grass. A Native American member of their team planned to lead the group in burning a smudge as part of worship the next day. One person raised his hand to indicate that he was allergic to sage smoke. The team member then said that they would burn sweet grass instead.

At this point another participant objected to the burning of anything at all. This participant explained convictions, stemming from her personal experience with spiritism, that such burning would only invite evil spirits into the room. Another participant explained that he too objected to this practice and requested that it not be allowed to continue.

The discussion then was joined by a variety of voices in the room. Some expressed concern about the smudging. Others supported it. In the end the staff facilitators left it up to the team planning the worship to decide how they would proceed.

Once the session ended, those objecting to the smudge approached the training staff to ask that the smudging not be allowed to take place under any circumstances. The staff responded by saying that they trusted the participant team to make the best decision possible and that they would support them in whatever they decided to do.

The participants as a whole and the training team itself was fairly well balanced between white people and people of color, women and men. Those objecting to the smudging included white people and people of color. The team proposing the smudge was also well-balanced racially.

During the course of the evening and into the night, the training team met as a group, met with the participant worship team, and observed a long discussion between the team with the most objections and some members of the worship team. Again white people and people of color were involved in all the discussions.

When meeting with the worship team, the event leaders again reiterated their support for whatever decision the team would make.

The following morning, the worship team informed the event leaders that they had chosen not to lead any worship at all. After intense discussions, the event leaders decided to open the meeting with the following statements:

> We support the decision made by the worship team. They had planned a worship experience that did what we asked them to do, "bring their cultural worship styles to the event." Among the Native American community in our church, there is not yet agreement on the appropriateness of indigenous worship styles. We will not decide it for them. We will not have a closing worship. Just a time of silence and a dismissal with prayer. Racism does not want us to proceed. We will not give into racism.

Soon after the event facilitators made the announcement, one participant left the room and did not return, another didn't say anything for the remainder of the training, and others were obviously made distraught by the experience. The event ended.

Iris's insight: No matter how many times I tell myself that to grow I must struggle with what I have known to be true and the new revelation God is trying to show me, it is still a difficult lesson to learn. Many times when I see people of color also struggling, I want to find some way to take away their discomfort. This maternal response is not unusual. The paradox in this thinking is that in my urge to protect, I end up hindering a person from her or his own personal growth. I learned this lesson again in the mid-West training.

In this conflict, the struggle among both the people of color groups was painful for all involved. One group wanted to hold on to what they knew as truth. The other team tried also to be faithful to what they knew as truth. As trainers, the question we were presented with was, "How do we minister to both groups while allowing both groups to struggle without rescuing or being maternal?"

As Tobin mentioned earlier, my gift is to see the bigger picture. I am able to see overall dynamics in the group setting. But what I learned is that my gift alone is powerless without the additional gifts of my colleagues. My reliance on my team members saved me from pushing my internal panic button that would have caused me to find some way to take away the discomfort. My team members also helped me reflect on how painful it is to be on both sides of such conflict.

The central lesson I learned was how, as a training team, we needed to hold each other accountable as we worked in the midst of racism-centered conflict. Christ incarnate was present in each one of us. I learned to appreciate Tobin's and Regina's gifts and was able to see how those gifts were woven together as a tapestry of God's love for each one of us. If we are faithful, God will be there to meet us in the midst of our struggle.

Tobin's take: The opportunity missed for white ally action in this story of sweet grass and sage is not so much an individual matter as a corporate one. What I most longed for in that setting is that one or more white person would have stood up and said, "This is not our discussion to control. The only possible group that could gain from whatever division is sowed among us is white people. Let's move into a time of caucusing."

Such a statement or proposal could have made it possible for people of color in the room to discuss their various experiences with a variety of worship styles, issues around colonialism and the devaluation of indigenous worship styles, and intergroup conflict. For white people, it would have availed us of the opportunity to explore how we can act so as not to gain from division among people of color. We could have also discussed how we set the primary standard by which all other worship forms are judged and our penchant to solve conflicts among groups of people of color for them.

With the benefit of hindsight, I can see the opportunity missed. For myself, I had to work hard simply not to run away. I long also for the spiritual strength to stay in the midst of such conflict, staying true to antiracist principles, and expecting the unexpected.

Ideas for action:

Discuss these questions:

1. Share stories of missed opportunities that you have been a part of. Note similarities and differences with the stories told here.
2. How do the insights about internalized racist oppression and superiority gleaned from the opening nine chapters color your reading of these stories? Where do you see evidence of internalized racist oppression or superiority?
3. Write down additional endings to the stories in this chapter. In what specific ways could the missed opportunities have been taken?
4. Is it possible to avoid making mistakes? What tools and principles can you identify for evaluating performances to learn what you can do better next time? Who should be the final assessor of those actions? Do people of color have a particular role to play in assessment of actions to dismantle racism?
5. These stories are shared from one perspective. What additional perspectives might have been missed? Can you imagine alternate versions of any of these stories from the perspective of others named? What information would you like to know in order to give life to alternate versions?

13

Opportunities Taken

God is our refuge and strength, a very present help in trouble.
(Psalm 46:1 NRSV)

In the last chapter we identified several times and places where white allies did not take the opportunities before them to engage in antiracist action. In this chapter we want to continue in a practical vein, but with more hope. Here we will examine times and places where white people and people of color were able to work together in effective solidarity to dismantle racism. We'll begin where we ended the last chapter, in the midst of a Midwest conflict.

Of sweet grass and sage reevaluated

Tobin's take two: I've already identified the elements of that complex conflict around sweet grass and sage that I wished were different. There are some elements that I thought were profoundly positive.

The first was that the team that was going to plan the worship involving the smudge demonstrated striking intra-team solidarity. At one point they made a clear choice about who should be talking with those objecting to their plans. White members were able to speak to other white people and people of color to other people of color. The team member made most vulnerable by the criticism was able to find time and space to gain strength because of the way the rest of the team drew around him.

I remember one team member had not expected the work of antiracism to be so difficult. In reply, another trainer noted, "Although the pain of racism may grow greater, God gives us deeper wells of strength to draw from as we struggle in response." I saw that team acknowledge the pain they were feeling but not stop or be silenced by it. In their work together, God did give them strength.

Their work as a team in their institution in the months that would follow required much more strength, probably more than they thought they had. From what I have heard, God continued to be strong among them.

The second area in which I saw much hope was the way in which our training team was able to struggle through our own uncertainties and, at least in my case, paralysis and fear. My inclination was to run as far away into that Midwest prairie as fast as I possibly could. I did not like conflict then. I do not like it now. I just wanted the problem to go away.

But it did not.

Yet, neither did my colleagues go away. Iris brought a fearless clarity about the dynamics in the room. She was able to identify the source of conflict and suggest a framework for responding. Regina's calm, spiritually centered perspective radiated out and calmed me in return. They were able to draw me back to the responsibility that I had to step up to. I was then able, alongside Regina, to stand in front of the group and say the truth that I had to speak. We were together able to say clearly that racism was seeking to destroy our work. We were together able to resist it.

The process of working through those painful times has prepared us collectively for facing other difficult conflicts that have since come among us. In the midst of working to dismantle racism, quite often the pain of racism does become greater. Yet, time and again, I have seen God provide wells of strength that only grow deeper and more refreshing.

Regina's reflection: I remember several things from the experience that were positive. The first thing is that the teams, including our own, had an opportunity to minister to each other in the midst of a crisis. This was validation to me of a process that seeks to nurture and care for people even as we uncover some ugly stuff.

People are often fearful of discussing difficult subjects because of the possibility of fracturing relationships. This is true when it comes to racism and antiracism work. Talking about the subject, we are told, will only invite dissent. But I witnessed relationships that had been merely cordial, and perhaps superficial, begin to deepen as folks grappled with this real-life situation in the midst of the training as teams. It was evident that it's possible to do this work and be the body of Christ: connected, serving various functions, and yet all working together.

Another positive was that how faith is expressed clearly mattered to everyone there. Something we had discussed only in theory, varying worship styles, was painfully present, and teams had to decide how to deal with it.

Likewise, our own team was greatly strengthened. By working together we were able to withstand personal attacks directed at us with grace and even a little humor. Because we were a team, when I needed to pull away, the others were there to keep the process moving.

Iris' insight again: In the midst of antiracism work, relationships often start out with a great degree of difficulty. Yet, we have seen some of the strongest bonds build among those groups that have worked hard together to dismantle racism. When we struggle, the relationships themselves grow stronger as well. Perhaps because we have struggled so often together, the bonds among our training team are also very strong.

And so, whenever difficulty arises at a training session, the natural thing to do as trainers is to stick together. At the

Midwest training, I think what we needed to do was go out among the participants. We needed to find ways to engage with them on a personal level, not to minimize the situation, but to be a companion on the journey. We needed to be that quiet and yet supportive presence. I have to admit this is very difficult for me because I would prefer to "fix" the conflict and get it over with as soon as possible. When working through difficult identity issues, as we do in antiracism work, we must move through the struggle—not escape from it.

Of course, God's work among us as we resist racism does not just take place in the Midwest or during antiracism trainings. Hope springs afresh in unexpected ways and in unlikely places elsewhere as well.

Changing the church

For the past five years, I (Regina) have served on the Mennonite Board of Congregational Ministries (MBCM), a program board of the Mennonite Church that provides resources to congregations. It is the most lively and challenging board I have ever served on. There is no rubber stamping here. I get great pleasure from working with what a former board member has aptly called a "feisty" group. We grapple seriously with each item brought to our table.

As a person of color in a largely white denomination, board service can be tricky. There are many questions to be considered: Am I here solely as a representative of "my people," or am I free to speak to all issues? Conversely, will I be the only one looking out for issues pertinent to me and my community? Will my issues be taken seriously or am I just a token, here to make the white board look more colorful and therefore more politically correct? Just how free am I to speak my mind? Rather than remaining silent wonderings, these very questions were frequently given voice around the MBCM table.

On the MBCM board, we have struggled with what it meant to become an antiracist entity in a virtually all-white church. In 1996, the staff went through antiracism training. Yet even prior to the training, before I came on the board, there was movement toward the ownership of such an identity. It seemed as though year after year, God had taken care to place articulate, passionate, and downright stubborn people on the board who wanted the church to be different in terms of its response to people of color.

A key point in the success of the endeavor came through the clearly articulated passion for antiracism from MBCM president Everett Thomas, a white man. Everett made known to the board and staff his love for Christ and the church while also sharing his understanding that a faithful witness to both need to include work against racism. Because of his commitment and his prominent position in the church, MBCM was able to make great strides in its antiracist movements. Over time, it became nearly automatic for *every* issue the board considered (not just ones specific to urban areas or directly concerning people of color) to include attention to what that decision would mean for people of color within our constituency and without.

Some of those decisions included:
- Raising funds for and promoting translation of Jubilee (children's Sunday school) curriculum into Spanish
- Making the biennial youth convention, the most public face of MBCM, more and more a place where youth of color feel they belong
- Beginning the process of providing culturally appropriate worship materials to congregations of color by spending time with leadership communities of color and inviting leadership of those communities to board meetings, at board expense
- Demanding accountability to people of color from other church institutions, including the denominational office. MBCM challenged these entities to make sure persons of color are at decision-making tables by suggesting 20 percent membership at the board level and at the executive committee level, and also used appointive power to

ensure that interagency groups have people of color in
their membership
- Hiring people of color
- Encouraging other program boards and the General
  Board to develop antiracism teams and have training
- Not depending upon resolutions and mere words on
  paper, but struggling through board meetings, conference
  calls, and ad hoc groups to make things happen
- Establishing the practice of a racism audit of board and
  staff

In order to make any of these things happen, white people had to give up power. White people had to listen to the
voices of people of color on the board, within the constituency, and from the outside. Staff had to change the way they
had worked for years in order to accommodate the above. It
did not happen overnight, but the staff and board came to
own an antiracist identity.

Everett also served on the steering committee for
Damascus Road. This was a personal decision for him, not
demanded by his position. Helpful for all the preceding agenda was Everett's high profile within the church, and his not
being afraid to use that profile to speak on behalf of the
antiracist agenda. He never operated in terms of "what we
white people need to do for those poor people of color," but
instead "we are the church together—how can we be faithful."

He also made himself vulnerable in the larger church on
behalf of the board. The board president, the staff, and white
board members not only gave up power, but used power in
appropriate ways. This is what needs to happen.

The MBCM board was also a good place for me to be on a
personal level. In addition to the hard work, there was time
built into our schedules to get to know one another personally. This increased the level of trust on the board and made it
possible to say hard things to one another when necessary.

Breaking the code

My (Tobin's) white, Mennonite upbringing has given me many gifts. It has also presented me with some hang-ups. One of those hang-ups is that I carry a great reticence to feeling simply and appropriately good about those times I have engaged in antiracist action that worked out well. My tendency is to ignore the story altogether and feign humility or overcompensate and tell the story with the swagger of smug success. I will try here to tell this story about a time that I was able to act in a manner consistent with antiracist principles.

Early on in my tenure at Mennonite Central Committee (MCC), members of the staff executive committee asked me to prepare a document examining what an affirmative action policy might look like in our setting. I spent several weeks working on the document, did careful research, and spoke with people of color within our organization asking for their feedback and direction.

I presented the document to the executive staff, all of whom were white. The one person of color at the executive level at that time was absent that day. I had anticipated some resistance, but the response I received confounded me in the depths of its overt racism. After a tumultuous and heated exchange, a decision was made to postpone the discussion until further work could be done.

That afternoon I sat down and wrote a memo to the executive committee members present at the staff meeting detailing what I had heard from them. Here is a quote from that memo:

> I am amazed that I heard what I did because I thought I was part of an organization that was willing to look clearly at the racism in our midst and respond humbly with change and new vision. If I am at all accurate in describing here what I have heard, I cannot continue in good conscience to recommend MCC as a safe, welcoming environment for my brothers and sisters from African-American, Latino, Asian, and Native American communities.

In the same breath, I must also identify the source of my paradoxical relief. It stems from a sense that maybe now we have moved beyond politeness and nicety. Maybe we can give up any pretense of being an organization concerned about working to dismantle our racism.

Perhaps that raw honesty will wake us up. I don't know.[1]

For better or worse, I then made a decision to carbon copy it to all people of color working within our headquarters' environment. Because I wanted to take full responsibility for my actions, I did not tell anyone I was going to do this until the memos were fully distributed.

To say the least, I received vociferous and detailed response. I had broken a code of silence and the response was deafening. Memos of response circled around for days afterwards. I was drawn to the desk of our executive director more than once and if not for her intervention would have clearly lost my job.

The result of the action was that an outside facilitator was brought in who was chosen by people of color in our organization. A meeting was held with the executive staff members and all people of color on staff who then articulated what they wanted to see happen. One of the outcomes was this statement in response to a document drafted by the executive committee:

> Your memo acknowledges that "MCC from its beginnings has been a statement about peace and reconciliation," and recognizes that "to be a peace organization it also has to be an antiracist organization." We agree. Our request was and is that these important qualities for being a Christian peace organization (racial justice, atonement, and reconciliation) be incorporated into MCC's mission statement. . . .
>
> We appreciate your willingness to hear our voices. We believe the integrity of MCC's efforts to be an agent of peace and reconciliation in communities around the

world is inextricably bound to MCC's commitment to be reconciled at home. We are committed to lovingly and peacefully pursue this broader vision for MCC in the Spirit of Jesus Christ.[2]

The primary feedback I received from people of color after that action was that what I did was dangerous and necessary. They also asked me to think about how I might have involved people of color even more directly in the preparatory process to begin with.

In hindsight, I think I did what was necessary in that setting. It wasn't fun. It involved significant pain. But I do think that out of this process many of us learned to trust each other at a much deeper level than we had ever before. Some of the cost of what is involved in this work became even more apparent and that was, perhaps, the greatest gift of all.

Institutional energy

Hope springs forth in unlikely places, even in institutions. The Mennonite Central Committee U.S. board is one place where I (Iris) have recently found hope. As a staff person and department head, I have frequent opportunities to engage with the board. Through our efforts to dismantle racism inside our institution, I have seen direct changes result.

One particularly important change has been that I now feel like my voice is being represented. By design, our board now includes a critical mass of people of color. As I sit and listen to the varied opinions expressed around the table, I hear new passion and commitments emerging. Even though white people have been concerned about immigration, there is now a real passion for finding ways to respond to the anti-immigrant sentiment. I'm not as sure if it would be as important if those voices where not present on the board. For us this has meant paying attention to issues south of the border but also for the Hmong and other Asian-American communities. Just as the Russian and Swiss Mennonites had personal connection with European immigrants, people of color on our board bring their personal connections to other immigrant communities.

We didn't get to this hopeful place by chance, however. We began with a commitment to diversity as expressed in a "Broadening the Vision" document and then took that commitment the next step by working to bring a critical mass of people of color to our staff and board. It took a real commitment from the executive office staff, even thought at times it was difficult.

The element that makes these changes sustainable and not just a function of a particular collection of personalities is that our new vision and structure document actually says that our identity is antiracist. This same structural document contains requirements that our board is diverse which makes it more than just a matter of good will or personal intent.

Those structural changes are then reflected in how the board operates. The discussion is quite animated. People of color speak freely about how they feel. In the midst of that discussion, it becomes apparent that people of color have various views. As is the reality for white people, one Asian-American or one African-American cannot speak for everyone.

Just as we had obstacles to overcome to get to this place, we also have significant challenges ahead. When forming our structural document, we struggled over whether or not to require percentages of people of color to be represented on the board. Some wanted to keep it as recommendation. People of color and white people were on both sides of the issue. In the end, we did keep required representation and it seems to be broadly owned. Now that we are such a diverse group, challenges ahead include seeing how we will prioritize programs, where we will spend money, and whose interests will be represented.

But I am left with hope. When I see a board like the one we now have, I see the beginning of a new thing. Multiple voices are being heard which gives me real hope for what will come out of the future programs we take on. It is exciting to think about the spectrum of possibilities now before us.

Closing

We chose to end this book by identifying a few ways in which we have seen people of color and white people working together as co-strugglers. In these stories, risks have been taken and some movement, however temporary or intangible, has taken place. As is often the case when working to dismantle racism, the people engaged in the struggle were not even aware of the movement forward until months or even years later. Every time the struggle was difficult and costly. Every time the struggle was Spirit-led.

We are convinced that it is possible for white people and people of color to work together as co-strugglers. We believe that this work requires educational and organizing skills. We also know that the best of our analysis, principles, experience, and sweat are nothing compared to the Spirit's voice nudging us to be ever more like Jesus.

May all our work to engage in a centuries' old tradition of resisting the powers that oppress be blessed by much endurance, all good boldness, wisdom, and the assurance that God will sustain us in the difficulty of this work. The longer we stay engaged in the task of dismantling racism, the more we are aware of how God does indeed sustain us. The work does not make us less thirsty, but as co-strugglers, the wells we drink from grow deeper.

Drink long. Drink deep. Go and be sustained.

Notes

Preface
1.   We are indebted to the work of Crossroads Ministry for introducing us to the ideas on which the following iceberg metaphor is based.

Chapter One
1   For children, skin color is just that, color. It is not a racial category.
2.   Carter Woodson's book *The Mis-education of the Negro* was originally published in 1933. It has since been republished by various publishers, the most recent being African American Images (2000).
3.   Lisa Page, "High Yellow White Trash," *Skin Deep: Black Women and White Women Write About Race*, Marita Golden and Susan Richards, eds. (New York: Doubleday, 1995), 14.
4.   bell hooks, *Black Looks: Race and Representation*, (Boston: South End Press, 1992), 3.
5.   William Peters, *A Class Divided, Then and Now*, (New Haven: Yale University Press, 1987), 108-9.

Chapter Four
1.   Marcus J. Borg, *Conflict, Holiness and Politics in the Teachings of Jesus*, (Harrisburg, Pa.: Trinity Press International, 1998), 12.
2.   Donna K. Bivens, "Internalized Racism: a definition," *Women Theological Center's Quarterly Newsletter*, June 1995.

Chapter Five
1.   Bivens, op cit.
2.   "Zero Tolerance and Racial Bias," *ColorLines*, Spring 2000, 32.

3.   Jack Forbes, *Columbus and Other Cannibals*, (New York: Autonomedia, 1992), 132.

Chapter Six

1.   Elizabeth Martinez, editor, *500 Years of Chicano History*, (Albuquerque, New Mexico: Southwest Organizing Project, 1991), i.

2.   Based on a presentation by Kimberly Richards at an anti-racism workshop by People's Institute for Survivial and Beyond, September 27-29, 1998.

3.   Richard L. Twiss, *Five Hundred Years of Bad Haircuts*, (Wiconi International, 1996), 21.

Chapter Seven

1.   Mark 12:18-34; 38-40. For this interpretation, I rely heavily on the work of Ched Myers in his insightful text *Binding the Strong Man: A Socio-Political Reading of the Gospel of Mark* (Orbis 1988).

2.   I am indebted to Zulma Prieto for the concept of "spaces" rather than "stages" to describe nonlinear developmental themes. While listed in an order that may suggest some level of sequential development, I use the term "spaces" to signify their interchangeable and nonsequential nature.

3.   In her book *Learning to Be White: Money, Race and God in America* (New York: Continuum, 1999), Thandeka tells multiple stories of white people being censured by their families, neighborhoods, schools, even churches when they moved outside appropriate boundaries of white behavior. She also relates her experience of challenging white people to use race specific language to describe themselves and other white people in informal conversation, i.e., "I was just saying to my white friend, Bob, the other day. . . ." Few take the challenge. Fewer still are able to do it for a week.

4.   Judith Levine, "White Like Me," *MS*, March/April 1994, 22.

Chapter Eight

1.   Thoughts I share here are heavily indebted to the work of Mab Segrest in *Memoir of a Race Traitor* (South End Press, 1994). Her essay "On Being White and Other Lies: A History of Racism in the United States" provides an excellent overview of the process of European peoples becoming white. See also Ronald Sanders, *Lost Tribes and Promised Lands: The Origins of American Racism* (New York: Harper & Row, 1992).

2. Howard Zinn, *A People's History of the United States* (New York: Harper & Row, 1980), 26-27, as quoted in Segrest, 189.

3. Segrest, 211.

4. Theodore Roosevelt, "The Winning of the West," in *Documents of American Prejudice: An Anthology of Writings on Race from Thomas Jefferson to David Duke*, ed. S. T. Joshi (New York: Basic Books, 1999), 137.

5. Amazon.com review of *Lies My Teacher Told Me*, "st_909@yahoo.com from Southern California, September 23, 1999, bring a bag, you may get sick to your stomach."

6. Segrest, 206-216.

7. Segrest, 195.

8. Segrest, 223.

9. Donelda Cook, "The Art of Survival in White Academia: Black Women Faculty Finding Where They Belong," in Michelle Fine, et al., *Off White: Readings on Race, Power and Society* (New York: Routledge, 1997), 102.

10. The short-lived sitcom "Dinosaurs" presents a fanciful, but all too real fable about this phenomenon in an episode entitled "Swamp Music."

11. Tim Wise, "Exploring the Depths of Racist Socialization," *Z Magazine*, July/August 1999, 18.

12. Thanks to Ched Myers for his helpful distinction between shame and guilt. For a more extensive treatment of the two concepts see Ched Myers, *Who Will Roll Away This Stone?: Discipleship Queries for First World Christians?* (Orbis 1994), 90-95.

13. Groot, 12.

14. Wise, 18.

15. Again, thanks to Myers as above.

16. Luzdy Stucky, November 5, 1999, in Akron, Pa.

Chapter Nine

1. Mark 12:39.

2. *A Common Place*, September 1995, "Let's Talk: Short-Term Service: Who Benefits?" Andrea Schrock Wenger.

3. Rose, Lillian Roybal, "White Identity and Counseling White Allies About Racism," *Bowser and Hunt*, 42.

4. Thompson, Becky, "Home/Work: Antiracism Activism and the Meaning of Whiteness," *Off White: Readings on Race, Power and Society*, Michelle Fine, et al., eds. (New York: Routledge, 1997), 361.

Chapter Ten
1. Langston Hughes, *Langston Hughes Reader: The Selected Writings of Langston Hughes*, (New York: George Braziller Inc., 1958), 181-182.
2. *Kaleidoscope of Justice*, vol. 1, no. 1, (Maine Council of Churches, 1996), 5.
3. Ibid.

Chapter Eleven
1. Karen McCabe-Juhnke, from e-mail sent 2/2/2000.
2. Bob Buxman, from e-mail sent 1/31/2000.
3. Marty Kelley, from e-mail sent 1/31/2000.
4. Ryan Good, from e-mail sent 1/17/2000.
5. Sharon Williams, from e-mail sent 1/13/2000.
6. Sylvia Shirk Charles, from e-mail sent 1/21/2000.
7. Phil Bergey, from e-mail sent 1/25/2000.
8. Daryl Byler, from e-mail sent 1/27/2000.
9. Buxman, 1/31/2000 e-mail.
10. McCabe-Juhnke, 2/2/2000 e-mail.
11. Everett Thomas, from e-mail sent 2/2/2000.
12. Betty Sommer, from e-mail sent 1/24/2000.
13. Byler, 1/27/2000 e-mail.
14. Jeanne Jantzi, from e-mail sent 1/21/2000.
15. Glenn Gilbert, from e-mail sent 2/3/2000.
16. Bergey, 1/25/200 e-mail.
17. Byler, 1/27/2000 e-mail.
18. Gilbert, 2/3/2000 e-mail.
19. Jantzi, 1/21/2000 e-mail.
20. Dody Matthias, from e-mail sent 1/27/2000.
21. Jacob has read this section and graciously given me permission to quote his poem and refer to him by his real name.

Chapter Thirteen
1. "Reflections on executive council meeting, " Jody Miller Shearer, September 7, 1995.
2. "Council's Response to 11/21 Meeting Discussion," Multiethnic staff, February 8, 1996.

Resources

Bivens, Donna K. "Internalized Racism: A definition." *Women's Theological Center's Quarterly Newsletter,* June 1995.

Borg, Marcus J. *Conflict, Holiness and Politics in the Teachings of Jesus.* Harrisburg, Pa.: Trinity Press International, 1998.

DeMott, Benjamin. *The Trouble with Friendship: Why Americans Can't Think Straight About Race.* New York: Atlantic Monthly, 1995.

Derman-Spark, Louise and Carol Brunson Phillips. *Teaching/Learning Anti-racism.* New York: Teachers College Press, 1997.

Dunn, James D. G. *Unity and Diversity in the New Testament,* 2nd ed. Valley Forge, Pa.: Trinity Press International, 1990.

Eng, Phoebe. *Warrior Lessions: An Asian American Women's Journey into Power.* New York: Pocket Books, 1999.

Fine, Michelle, et al., eds. *Off White: Readings on Race, Power, and Society.* New York: Routledge, 1997.

Forbes, Jack. *Columbus and Other Cannibals.* New York: Autonomedia,1992.

Frankenberg, Ruth. *White Women, Race Matters: The Social Construction of Whiteness.* Minneapolis: University of Minnesota, 1993.

hooks, bell. *Black Looks.* Boston: South End Press, 1992.

Martinez, Elizabeth, editor. *500 Years of Chicano History.* Albuquerque, New Mexico: Southwest Organizing Project, 1991.

Neyrey, Jerome H. "Clean/Unclean, Pure/Polluted, and Holy/Profane: The Idea and System of Purity." *The Social Sciences and New Testament Interpretation.* R. L. Rohrbaugh, ed. Peabody, Mass.: Hendrickson, 1996.

Page, Lisa. "High Yellow White Trash." *Skin Deep: Black Women and White Women Write About Race.* Marita Golden and Susan Richards Shreve eds. New York: Doubleday, 1995.

Shearer, Jody Miller. *Enter the River: Healing Steps from White Privilege Toward Racial Reconciliation.* Scottdale, Pa.: Herald Press, 1994.

Tatum, Beverly Daniel. *"Why Are All the Black Kids Sitting Together in the Cafeteria?" And Other Conversations About Race.* New York: Basic Books, 1997.

Twiss, Richard L. *Five Hundred Years of Bad Haircuts.* Wiconi International, 1996.

Wink, Walter. *Naming the Powers.* Philadelphia: Fortress Press, 1984.

———. *Unmasking the Powers.* Philadelphia: Fortress Press, 1986.

———. *Engaging the Powers.* Minneapolis: Fortress Press, 1992.

"Zero Tolerance and Racial Bias." *ColorLines,* Spring 2000, 32.

Conrad Moore

The Authors

Iris de León-Hartshorn is the director of the Peace and Justice Ministries Department of Mennonite Central Committee U.S. Iris lives in Lancaster, Pennsylvania, with her husband, Leo Hartshorn. They are the parents of three children.

Regina Shands Stoltzfus is the associate pastor at Lee Heights Community Church in Cleveland, Ohio. She is the cofounder of Damascus Road and has worked with Mennonite Central Committee and the Ohio Conference of the Mennonite Church. Regina is married to Art Stoltzfus and the coparent of four children.

Tobin Miller Shearer is the cofounder of Damascus Road antiracism process. He is author of the book *Enter the River* and several antiracism youth curriculums. Tobin is husband to Cheryl and father of Dylan and Zachary.